DR. DOBSON'S
Handbook *of*
Family
Advice

DR. DOBSON'S
Handbook *of*
Family
Advice

Encouragement and Practical
Help for Your Home

Dr. James Dobson

HARVEST HOUSE PUBLISHERS
EUGENE, OREGON

Scripture quotations are taken from The Holy Bible, *New International Version*® *NIV*®. Copyright ©
1973, 1978, 1984, 2011 by Biblica, Inc.™ Used by permission. All rights reserved worldwide.

Cover by Koechel Peterson & Associates, Inc., Minneapolis, Minnesota

Author photos by Harry Langdon: harrylangdon.com

Adapted from two previously published books: *Home with a Heart: Encouragement for Families* and
Coming Home: Timeless Wisdom for Families.

DR. DOBSON'S HANDBOOK OF FAMILY ADVICE
Copyright © 1996/1998 by Dr. James C. Dobson, PhD
Published by Harvest House Publishers
Eugene, Oregon 97402
www.harvesthousepublishers.com

Library of Congress Cataloging-in-Publication Data
Dobson, James C., 1936-
Dr. Dobson's handbook of family advice / James Dobson.
p. cm.
Adapted from: Home with a heart. Wheaton, Ill.: Tyndale House Publishers, c1996. Coming
home. Wheaton, Ill.: Tyndale House, c1998.
Includes bibliographical references (p.) and index.
ISBN 978-0-7369-4373-4 (pbk.)
ISBN 978-0-7369-4374-1 (eBook)
1. Families—Religious life. 2. Parenting—Religious aspects—Christianity. 3. Christian life.
I. Dobson, James C., 1936- Home with a heart. II. Dobson, James C., 1936- Coming home. III.
Title. IV. Title: Doctor Dobson's handbook of family advice. V. Title: Handbook of family advice.
BV4526.3.D63 2012
248.4—dc23
                                                                    2012002087

Printed in the United States of America

12 13 14 15 16 17 18 19 20 / LB-SK / 10 9 8 7 6 5 4 3 2 1

CONTENTS

INTRODUCTION

Thank you for your interest in this book, which we have titled *Dr. Dobson's Handbook of Family Advice*. It is a compilation of many of my favorite commentaries addressing the subjects of children; marriage; teenagers; grandparents; single parents; public, private, and home schools; blended families; medical research; and dozens of related topics. I hope you'll find these suggestions helpful and practical for your own home.

The concepts and ideas included in this book were drawn from hundreds of radio and television commentaries aired throughout the United States and in more than 100 other countries on six continents. The listening audience is estimated to be in excess of 220 million people every day.

How do we explain such broad interest in family-related topics among the peoples of the world? This appetite for information is a relatively recent development. What we are observing now, however, is that millions of husbands and wives are concerned about the enormous challenges that are plaguing the institutions of marriage and parenthood. Indeed, the human family is a small community that is facing universal problems, including divorce, drugs, infidelity, juvenile delinquency, violence, and many other difficulties. This appears to explain why families in diverse cultures are suddenly receptive to timeless advice that is based on the wisdom of the Judeo-Christian system of values.

The commentaries you are about to read were written in a 90-second format, which makes them concise and to the point. I think you will enjoy them. Some are practical. Some are spiritual. Some are serious. Some are humorous. And some are intended simply to inspire the "better angels" within us. In the end, each commentary is designed to make its own small contribution to the relationships that matter most—those that thrive in the home.

I believe these statements will hit close to where you live. Greetings to you and your family.

—James C. Dobson, PhD
Founder and President of Family Talk
Colorado Springs, Colorado 80907

1

BOUNDARIES

The Security of Boundaries

Children feel more secure, and therefore tend to flourish, when they know where the boundaries are. Let me illustrate that principle.

Imagine you're driving a car over the Royal Gorge Bridge in Colorado, which is suspended hundreds of feet above the canyon floor. As a first-time traveler, you're pretty tense as you drive across. It is a scary experience. I knew one little fellow who was so awed by the view over the side of the bridge that he said, "Wow, Daddy! If you fell off of here, it'd kill you constantly!"

Now suppose there were no guardrails on the side of the bridge. Where would you steer the car? Right down the middle of the road. Even though you don't plan to hit those protective railings along the side, you just feel more secure knowing that they're there.

It's the same way with children. There is security in defined limits. They need to know precisely what the rules are and who's available to enforce them. When these clear boundaries exist at home, the child lives in utter safety. He never gets in trouble unless he deliberately asks for it. And as long as he stays within those reasonable, well-marked guardrails, there's mirth and freedom and acceptance.

Your children need the security of defined limits, too. They may not admit that they want you to be the boss, but they breathe easier when you are.

Mom's Football Team

In the late 1960s, the phrase "If it feels good, do it" made its way around the counterculture. It meant, in effect, that a person's flighty impulses should be allowed to overrule every other consideration. "Don't think—just follow your heart" was the prevailing attitude. That foolish advice has ruined many gullible people. Those who ignore lurking dangers are casting themselves adrift in the path of life's storms. We must be prepared to disregard ephemeral feelings at times and govern our behavior with common sense.

Not only can emotions be dangerous—they can also be unreliable and foolish. I'm reminded of a story told by my mother about her high school years. They had one of the worst football teams in the history of Oklahoma. They hadn't won a game in years. Finally a wealthy oil producer asked to speak to the team in the locker room and offered a brand-new Ford to every boy and to each coach if they would simply defeat their bitter rivals in the next game. The team went crazy. For seven days they thought about nothing but football. They couldn't even sleep at night. Finally the big night arrived, and the team was frantic with anticipation. They assembled on the sidelines, put their hands together, and shouted, "Rah!" Then they ran onto the field—and were smashed thirty-eight to nothing. No amount of excitement could compensate for the players' lack of discipline, conditioning, practice, study, coaching, drill, experience, and character. Such is the nature of emotion. It has a definite place in human affairs but is not a substitute for intelligence, preparation, and self-control.

Instead of responding to your impulses, therefore, it is often better to hang tough when you feel like quitting, to guard your tongue when you feel like talking, to save your money when you feel like spending, and to remain faithful when you feel like flirting. Unbridled feelings will get you in trouble nine times out of ten.

So, before you chase after something that simply feels good, you might want to think it over. You could be about to make one of your greatest blunders.

Children and Materialism

It's not easy to say no to children, especially in an affluent and permissive society. Toy companies are spending millions of dollars on advertising aimed at children—not their parents. They know boys and girls are the very best customers. But by giving in to this pressure, parents may actually deprive their children of pleasure. Here's why.

Pleasure occurs when an intense need is met. A glass of water is worth more than gold to a person who's dying of thirst, but it's worthless to the person who doesn't need it. That principle applies directly to children. If you never allow a boy or girl to desire something, he or she will not fully enjoy the pleasure of receiving it. If you give him a tricycle before he can walk, and a bike before he can ride, and a car before he can drive, and a diamond ring before he knows the value of money, you may actually have deprived him of the satisfaction he could have received from that possession.

How unfortunate is the child who never has the opportunity to long for something, to dream about that prize by day, and to plot for it by night, perhaps even to get desperate enough to work for it.

Excessive materialism is not only harmful to children—but it deprives them of pleasure, too.

Children and Television

There's been considerable debate in recent years about television rating systems. That kind of information is desperately needed by parents who want to protect their kids from harmful content, and I'm among those who believe that the present system just doesn't get the job done.

But even if changes are implemented, there's a new wrinkle to be considered. Social research conducted by Yankelovich Partners, Inc., has analyzed the television-viewing habits of Americans. What they discovered is surprising. Forty-two percent of children between nine and seventeen have their own cable or satellite television hookups in their bedrooms.[1] The image of families gathered around a single TV set in the family room is fading. Instead, many kids are off by themselves where they can choose anything that they want to see.

Ann Clurman, a partner at Yankelovich, said, "Almost everything children are seeing is essentially going into their minds in some sort of uncensored or unfiltered way."[2] Considering the explicit sex, violence, nudity, and profanity available now, especially on cable and satellite television, this is a disturbing revelation.

Children need to be protected from adult programming, and yet almost four out of every ten kids have parents who don't really know what they're watching. I fear that situation will come back to haunt us for years to come.

2

COMMUNICATION

Learning to Communicate Feelings

You talk and talk, but your partner just doesn't seem to comprehend. Have you ever had that experience? Well, maybe it's time you tried a new form of communication.

One very effective way to express your feelings is to paint a word picture. My good friends Gary Smalley and John Trent described this technique in their book *The Language of Love.* They told of a woman who was feeling frustrated because her husband would come home from work and clam up. He had nothing to say all evening. Finally, his wife told him a story about a man who went to breakfast with some friends. He ate a big meal, and then he gathered up some crumbs and put them in a bag. Then he went to lunch with some business associates and ate a big steak. Again, he put a few of the crumbs in a bag to take home. When he came home that night, he handed his wife the little bag of leftovers. The woman told her husband, "That's what you are doing to me. All day the children and I wait to talk with you when you get home. But you don't share yourself with us. After being gone all day, you hand us a doggie bag and turn on the television set." The husband said hearing it put this way was like being hit with a two-by-four. He apologized and began to work on opening himself to his wife and family.

Word pictures. They are far more effective than a tornado of hostile words.

The First Five Minutes

I heard about a brilliant but simple principle some years ago that I never forgot. Its thesis was based on the concept of "the first five minutes," describing the way people relate to each other. Everything they do for hours is influenced by the first moments they spend together.

For example, a speaker is given very few moments to convince his audience that he really does have something worthwhile to say. If he's boring or stilted in the beginning, his listeners will begin thinking about something else, and the orator will never understand why. If he hopes to use humor during his speech, he'd better say something funny very quickly, or his audience won't believe he can make them laugh. The opportunity of the moment is lost.

Closer to home, the first five minutes of a morning determine how a mother will interact with her children on that day. A snarl or a complaint as the kids gather for breakfast will sour their relationship for hours.

And when a man arrives home from work at the end of the day, the way he greets his wife will influence their interaction throughout the evening. If he mutters, "Not tuna casserole again!" the relationship will be put on edge from then to bedtime.

Fortunately, when we have been apart from those we love, we have an opportunity to reset the mood. A little sensitivity when coming back together can produce surprising benefits. It all depends on the first five minutes.

Differing Assumptions

One of the most common sources of conflict between husbands and wives comes down to a simple matter of differing assumptions. Let me illustrate. Some years ago I went through a very hectic period of my life professionally. I was a full-time professor in a medical school, but I was also traveling and speaking far more often than usual. I completely exhausted myself during that time. It was a dumb thing to do, but I had made commitments that I simply had to keep.

Finally on a concluding Friday night the siege was over, and I came dragging home. I had earned a day off, and I planned to kick back and watch a USC–Alabama football game that Saturday. Shirley, on the other hand, also felt that she had paid her dues. For six weeks she had taken care of the kids and run the home. It was entirely reasonable that I spend my Saturday doing things she wanted done around the house. Neither of us was really wrong. Both had a right to feel as we did. But the two ideas were incompatible.

Those assumptions collided about ten o'clock Saturday morning when Shirley asked me to clean the backyard umbrella. I had no intention of doing it. There was an exchange of harsh words that froze our relationship for three days.

It's important to understand that neither of us was looking for a fight, yet we both felt misunderstood and wounded by the other. Our conflict was typical of what goes on every day in a million other homes. It all comes down not to deliberate antagonism but to something called "differing assumptions."

We can avoid most of these clashes simply by making sure that the two people know what is on the other's mind. They might still disagree, but the unpleasant surprises can be prevented.

The Apology

Have you ever found the courage to say "I'm sorry" to a child? It is difficult to do, and my father was never very good at it. I remember working with him in the backyard when I was fifteen years of age, on a day when he was particularly irritable for some reason. He crabbed at me for everything I did, even though I tried to please him. Finally, he yelled at me for something petty, and I had had enough. I threw down the rake and quit. Defiantly, I walked across our property and down the street as my dad demanded that I come back. It was one of the few occasions I ever took him on like that!

I meandered around town for a while, wondering what would happen to me when I finally went home. I ended up at my cousin's house on the other side of town. After several hours there, I admitted what I had done, and my uncle urged me to phone. With knees quaking, I called my dad.

"Stay there," he said. "I'm coming over."

To say that I was scared would be an understatement. Dad arrived in a short time and asked to see me alone.

"Bo," he began, "I didn't treat you right this afternoon. I was riding your back for no good reason, and I'm sorry. Your mom and I want you to come home now."

It was a tough moment for him, but he made a friend for life. And in so doing, he taught me something about apologizing that would someday be useful to me as a father.

The Fine Art of Conversation

Are you tired of those one-word answers your child or teenager gives in response to your questions? You ask how well he played in soccer practice, and he says, "Fine." You wonder how he got along in school today, and he says, "OK." End of the "dialogue."

Well, I have a suggestion that may help. I ran across a simple but very effective way to teach children the art of conversation. It was included in an article written by Sybil Ferguson in *Woman's Day*. I've taught this technique to my own children and hope you will find it helpful, too.

Give three tennis balls to your daughter, and ask her to throw them back one at a time. Instead of returning the balls, however, simply hold them. Your daughter will stand there looking at you awkwardly and wondering what to do next. Obviously, it isn't much of a game. Then you explain that good conversation is like that game of catch. One person throws an idea or a comment to the other, and he or she tosses it back. Talking to each other is simply a matter of throwing ideas back and forth.

For example, if you ask your daughter, "How did it go in school today?" and she answers, "Fine," she has caught the ball and held it. We have nothing more to say to each other. But if she responds, "I had a good day because I got an A on my history test," she has caught the ball and thrown it back. I can then ask, "Was it a difficult test?" or "Did you study hard for it?" or "I'll bet you're proud of yourself."[1]

To teach your children how to communicate, simply show them how to catch and throw. Even a very young child can understand that idea. It's just a matter of playing the game.

A Better Way of Moving On

Moving to a new school or a new city can be a threatening experience for children, but there are some ways to make the transfer easier.

Preparation and forethought are the keys. Educator Cheri Fuller recommends that those who are about to relocate call a family meeting to talk about what's about to happen. Begin to lay plans together. It's sad to say good-bye to good friends, and it's hard to make new ones. Try establishing pen pals for your children in the new school long before the move is to occur. Relationships can blossom through the mail so that the kids are not entirely unknown in the new location.

It's also good to create curiosity about the new city or neighborhood you're moving to. Write to the state tourist bureau or to the chamber of commerce and ask for brochures and maps. When your children begin to see some of the adventure of moving, they may develop a more positive attitude toward leaving.

A bit of preparation and a healthy dose of communication can help clear the way for a smoother journey to a new home.

Families at the Dinner Table

Dr. Blake Bowden and his colleagues at the Cincinnati Children's Hospital Center studied 527 teenagers to learn what family and lifestyle characteristics were related to mental health and adjustment. Their findings were significant.

What they found is that adolescents whose parents ate dinner with them five times per week or more were the least likely to be on drugs, to be depressed, or to be in trouble with the law. They were more likely to be doing well in school and to be surrounded by a supportive circle of friends. Surprisingly, the benefit was seen even for families that didn't eat together at home. Those who met at fast-food restaurants had the same result. By contrast, the more poorly adjusted teens ate with their parents only three evenings per week or less.

What do these findings mean? Is there something magic about sitting down together over a meal? No, and those parents who interpret the conclusions that way will be disappointed. What Bowden's study shows is that adolescents do far better in school and in life when their parents are *involved* with them—when they have time for them—and specifically, when they get together almost every day for conversation and interaction. [2]

Study after study has emphasized that same message. Families are critically important to the well-being of children.

3

COMMUNITY AND COMPASSION

Our Civic Duty

We live under a representative form of government which Abraham Lincoln described as being "of the people, by the people, and for the people." Unfortunately, not enough of us take the time to let our representatives know how we really feel about issues that concern us.

Letters and phone calls to our local officials, representatives, and senators do make a difference, and these people certainly need to hear from us. Let me offer a few ideas that may help in making your letter the most effective it can be. First, be brief, and restrict each letter to one subject or one piece of legislation. This makes it easier for the recipient to respond and for his or her staff to organize correspondence. If the letter is about a specific bill, identify it by name and number. Second, make your letter personal. Form letters and postcards do have a place, but personal letters get more attention. Describe how the proposed bill or course of action would affect you or your family or your community. Give the essential background information as well. And third, remember that elected officials receive thousands of letters of complaint and very few positive responses.

If a public official says or does something that you like, respond with a quick note of appreciation, and by all means, remember that democracy works best when the people make their wants and wishes known.

A Simple Bag of Groceries

A few years ago I slipped into a market to buy a few groceries for lunch. Standing in front of me at the checkout was an elderly woman who didn't seem to be altogether lucid. It quickly became obvious that she had selected more food than she could pay for, as she fumbled in her purse frantically for a few more coins. The checker politely continued to add up the items.

"I just don't understand where my money is," said the old lady as she made another desperate foray into the depths of her purse.

With that, I whispered to the checker, "Just go ahead and total her bill. Accept whatever money she has and put the rest on my bill."

That's what she did, and I paid an extra eight dollars to make up the difference. The old woman never knew that I had helped her. She shuffled off with her cart, relieved that her groceries had cost exactly the amount of money she was able to locate. Then I looked back at the checker and saw that she was crying. I asked her why.

"Because," she said, "I've been doing this work for twenty years, and I've never seen anyone do something like that before."

It was no big deal—an insignificant eight dollars—but simple kindness is so unusual today that it shocks us when it occurs. I'll tell you this: That may have been the best eight dollars I ever spent! I only wish I'd paid the rest of the dear lady's bill.

Helping a Single Mom

Many years ago, my wife, Shirley, was working around the house one morning when a knock came at the front door. When she opened it, there stood a young woman in her late teens who called herself Sally.

"I'm selling brushes," she said, "and I wonder if you'd like to buy any."

Well, my wife told her she wasn't interested in buying anything that day, and Sally said, "I know. No one else is, either." And with that, she began to cry.

Shirley invited Sally to come in for a cup of coffee, and she asked her to share her story. She turned out to be an unmarried mother who was struggling mightily to support her two-year-old son. That night, we went to her shabby little apartment above a garage to see how we could help this mother and her toddler. When we opened the cupboards, there was nothing there for them to eat, and I mean nothing. That night, they both dined on a can of SpaghettiOs. We took her to the market, and we did what we could to help get her on her feet.

Sally is obviously not the only single mother out there who is desperately trying to survive in a very hostile world. All of these mothers could use a little kindness—from babysitting to providing a meal to repairing the washing machine or even to just showing a little thoughtfulness.

Raising kids all alone is the toughest job in the universe. Do you suppose there's someone in your neighborhood who is going down for the third time? How about giving her a helping hand? Not only will it bring encouragement to the mother, but one or more children will bless you as well.

Respect for the Elderly

M any years ago I saw a documentary television program that I never forgot. It focused on the life of an elderly woman named Elizabeth Holt Hartford, who lived alone in a Los Angeles slum. These were her parting words that were aired on videotape a few weeks after her death:

> You see me as an old lady who's all broken down with age. But what you don't understand is that this is me in here. I'm trapped in a body that no longer serves me. It hurts, and it's wrinkled and diseased. But I haven't changed. I'm still the person I used to be when this body was young.

Those who are younger may find it difficult to appreciate Mrs. Hartford's words. She was speaking of the "Unwanted Generation" and what it is like to be aged in a time dominated by the very young; to be unable to see or hear well enough; to have an active mind that is hopelessly trapped in an inactive body; to be dependent on busy children; to be virtually sexless, emotionally and physically, in an eroticized society; to be unable to produce or contribute anything really worthwhile; and to have no one who even remembers your younger days.

A gastroenterologist once told me that 80 percent of his older patients have physical symptoms caused by emotional problems. Despair is quickly translated into bodily disorders. Obviously, self-worth is essential to well-being at all ages. Let's extend our love and respect to those such as Elizabeth Holt Hartford who have passed their prime.

Dear Friends and Gentle Hearts

On an icy January morning many years ago, a man was found naked and bleeding in a twenty-five-cent-a-night flophouse. Doctors sewed up the gash in his throat as best they could, but the wound and the booze had taken their toll. That night he died in his sleep.

A nurse gathering his belongings found a dirty coat with only thirty-eight cents in one pocket and a scrap of paper in the other, on which five words were written: "Dear friends and gentle hearts." *Almost like the words of a song,* she thought. And she was right. This old man turned out to have been the songwriter who penned some of America's most beloved music, including "Swanee River," "Oh! Susanna!" "My Old Kentucky Home," and hundreds more. He was Stephen Foster.[1]

That true story comes to mind whenever I see a derelict—a down-and-outer—on the street today. That dirty, sotted man or woman wasn't always in that condition. He or she was once a little baby, bubbling with promise and hope—before being cut down by the pruning knife of time. A wrong choice or two—an unfortunate circumstance at a critical moment—led to the tragedy of a wasted life.

It's difficult to see beyond a bleary-eyed bum sleeping on a park bench today, but there is a person of value within that exterior. He or she might be another creative genius at the end of a long and bitter journey.

Togetherness

L et me ask you to take in a deep breath of air and hold it for a moment. Then exhale it. You might be interested to know that this single breath of air contains at least three nitrogen atoms that were inhaled by every person who has ever lived, including Leonardo da Vinci, Winston Churchill, and Abraham Lincoln. Likewise, each of the dinosaurs in their time breathed some of the same nitrogen atoms that you took into your body. And the air that you just exhaled will circle the globe in the next twelve months, and everyone will breathe at least one or two of those individual atoms.

That scientific fact dramatizes the connectedness between us as human beings. Just as we share our chemistry with other members of the human family, we are all interdependent socially. We are affected positively or negatively by the actions of each other. During the self-centered days of what used to be called the "me" generation, it was common to hear people say, "As long as I'm not hurting anyone, it's nobody's business what I do." Unfortunately, everything we do affects other people, and there's no such thing as a completely independent act.

The poet John Donne wrote, "No man is an island, entire of itself, every man is a piece of a continent, a part of the main."[2] How true were his words.

4

CONFIDENCE THROUGH ENCOURAGEMENT

A Star in the Apple

Some parents refer to their children as the apple of their eye, but one mom I know affectionately thinks of her kids as the "star in the apple."

This mother discovered one day that by cutting an apple horizontally across the middle, instead of coring it and slicing it in wedges from top to bottom, something new and striking appeared. A perfect five-point star was formed by the tiny seeds at the center. The star had been there all along, of course, but she'd just never seen it before because she always approached the apple from a different point of view.

There's an analogy to children here that intrigues me. Most of us look at these little creatures we call kids in a certain way year after year. We see them perhaps as lazy or irritating or demanding. But children are infinitely complex, and we may be overlooking qualities of character that we've never seen before. We could be missing the "star" at the heart of these young lives.

If we try to see them through fresh eyes every now and then, we may stumble onto a whole new wonderful dimension to their personalities that escaped us before. So give it a try! Begin looking at your children from a new angle.

There is, I promise, a star tucked away inside every boy and girl.

The Lollipop

A mother named Elaine told me a very moving story about her three-year-old daughter, Beth, who was the youngest child in their neighborhood. She toddled after the big kids but understood that they didn't really want her along.

One day this mother looked out her kitchen window and saw Beth standing at a fence, watching the other children playing baseball. They wouldn't let her play, of course, and it was upsetting her. Suddenly, the little girl turned and ran into the house calling, "Lollipop, Mom! I need lollipop!"

Elaine went to the cupboard and handed the child a lollipop.

"No! No, Mommy," Beth said. "I want lots of lollipops."

The mother knew something was up, so she gave the child an armload of lollipops. Beth then ran back to her place at the fence and stood there silently, holding the lollipops out to the other children. She was trying to buy their acceptance—but they didn't notice her. Finally, one of the bigger kids saw Beth and yelled to the others. They ran over and grabbed the treats away from the toddler and then went back to play without even thanking her. Elaine stood watching at the window with a lump in her throat. The gifts were gone—and so were Beth's friends.

How many insecure teenagers give everything they have—including their own bodies—to gain acceptance from their peers? Then they are left standing at the fence, alone and rejected—with their lollipops gone. These are among the most painful experiences of a lifetime—for adolescents *and* for their parents. There are times when moms and dads can do nothing to help their children except to stand at the window, praying that God will get them through it!

Mistaken Identity

Jaime Escalante, the Garfield High School teacher on whom the movie *Stand and Deliver* was based, once told me this story about a fellow teacher. During his first year in the classroom, he had two students named Johnny. One was a happy child, an excellent student, a fine citizen. The other Johnny spent much of his time goofing off and making a nuisance of himself.

When the PTA held its first meeting of the year, a mother came up to this teacher and asked, "How's my son, Johnny, getting along?" He assumed she was the mom of the better student and replied, "I can't tell you how much I enjoy him. I'm so glad he's in my class."

The next day the problem child came to the teacher and said, "My mom told me what you said about me last night. I haven't ever had a teacher who wanted me in his class."

He completed his assignments that day and brought in his completed homework the next morning. A few weeks later, the problem Johnny had become one of this teacher's hardest-working students—and one of his best friends. This misbehaving child's life was turned around all because he was mistakenly identified as a good student.

Not every lazy or underachieving boy or girl could be motivated by a simple compliment from a teacher, of course, but there is a principle here that applies to all kids: It's better to make a child stretch to reach your high opinion than stoop to match your disrespect.

Flattery Versus Praise

I t is good to praise children for the responsible things they do, but should there be a limit to the compliments we offer them?

Affirmation is essential to children's self-esteem, and they develop best when they get plenty of it. But too many good words heaped on kids for the wrong reasons can be inflationary and unhealthy for them. This empty rhetoric is called flattery, which differs from praise in that it is unearned. Flattery is what Grandma offers when she comes for a visit and says, "Oh, what a beautiful little girl you are! You're getting prettier every day," or, "My, what a smart boy you are. Aren't you big?"

Let me say it again. Flattery occurs when compliments are showered on a child for something that is unrelated to effort, achievement, or maturity. Praise, on the other hand, is a genuine reaction to the good things that a child has done.

To be effective, praise should be very specific. "You've been a good boy" is too general. Much better is "I like the way you cleaned your room today" or "I'm proud of the way you studied for that math assignment last night." You see, praise reinforces the child's constructive behavior. It rewards him or her for doing something positive and valuable and increases the chances that it will recur.

As parents, we should be on the lookout for opportunities to offer genuine, well-deserved praise to our children while avoiding the emptiness of flattery.

That's OK, Jake

Dick Korthals, one of our volunteers at Focus on the Family, described his experience while attending a dog show. As part of the competition, a dozen dogs were commanded to "Stay!" and then expected to remain statuelike for eight minutes while their owners left the ring. Judges scored them on how well they were able to hold their composure during their master's absence.

About four minutes into the exercise, Dick noticed a magnificent German shepherd named Jake sitting at the end of the line. It became apparent immediately that he was losing his poise, slinking slowly toward the ground. By the time his trainer returned, poor Jake was lying flat on his stomach with his head on his paws.

Jake saw the disappointment in his owner's eyes and began crawling toward him on his belly. Everyone was expecting the trainer to scold the dog for his poor performance. Instead, he bent down, cupped the dog's head in his hands, and said with a smile, "That's OK, Jake. We'll do better next time." It was a very touching moment.[1]

There's a lesson here for every parent, too. It's inevitable that our children will disappoint us. Our natural reaction when they fail is to bark at them, saying, "Why didn't you do it right?!" and, "How could you have been so stupid?!" But if we're wise, we'll remember their immaturity and imperfection.

That is the moment to say with a hug, "That's OK, my child. We'll do better next time."

5

CONFLICT

Letting Children Express Anger

Children inevitably become angry with their parents from time to time. Should they be allowed to express that emotion, and if so, precisely how?

If a child is prohibited from expressing his or her negative frustrations toward mother or father, that individual will often vent those feelings through what psychologists call "passive aggression." Maybe he'll pout or wet the bed or get bad grades in school. Perhaps she'll become depressed or eat too much. Usually children aren't aware that these behaviors are being fueled by anger. The behaviors are simply unconscious ways of expressing accumulated hostility toward parents.

It *is* important, therefore, to allow children to vent anger when it is intense. On the other hand, I firmly believe that they should also be taught to be respectful to their parents. It is not appropriate to permit name-calling, back talk, or sassiness and disrespect. Instead, children should be assured that they can say anything to their parents, including very negative feelings, as long as it's expressed in a respectful manner.

For example, "You embarrassed me in front of my friends," or, "I don't think I got my fair share," or, "Sometimes I think you love Billy more than me." Those are appropriate responses. "I hate you" and "You are so stupid!" are not acceptable retorts.

By following this general guideline, we're teaching children how to deal with anger in appropriate ways. That skill might come in handy with a future husband or wife.

Learning to Fight Fair

Since conflict exists in every romantic relationship, learning to fight fair just might be the most important lesson a couple can master.

The first obligation is to understand the difference between healthy and unhealthy combat in marriage. In an unstable marriage, hostility is aimed at the partner's soft underbelly with comments like "You never do anything right!" and "Why did I marry you in the first place?" and "You're getting more like your mother every day!" These offensive remarks strike at the very heart of the mate's self-worth.

Healthy conflict, by contrast, remains focused on the issues that cause disagreement. For example: "It upsets me when you don't tell me you're going to be late for dinner," or "I was embarrassed when you made me look foolish at the party last night." Can you hear the difference?

Even though the two approaches may be equally contentious, the first assaults the dignity of the partner while the second addresses the source of conflict. When couples learn this important distinction, they can work through their disagreements without wounding and insulting each other.

Basic civility is one of the building blocks of lifelong marriage.

Power Games

Have you noticed that family members can become world-class experts at manipulating one another?

Deep within the human spirit is the desire for raw power. We want to run our own lives and everyone else's, if we can. There are dozens of techniques that people commonly use to control those around them. Among them are...

- Emotional blackmail: "Do what I want or I'll get very angry and go all to pieces."

- The guilt trip: "How could you do this to me after I've done so much for you?"

- The eternal illness: "Don't upset me. Can't you see I'm sick?"

- Help from beyond the grave: "Your dear father would've agreed with me."

- Divine revelation: "God told me you should do what I want."

- The humiliation: "Do what I want or I'll embarrass you at home and abroad."

These are powerful tools that are used every day in getting others to dance to a different tune. Not only are adults good at using them, but teenagers can be masters of manipulation. Their techniques include teenage terror: "Leave me alone or I'll pull a stupid adolescent stunt (suicide, alcohol, drugs, and so on)," or fertile follies: "Do what I want or I'll present you with a baby." That threat unravels the nerves of every adult.

Manipulation is a game any number can play—right in the privacy of your own home. But those who engage in it pay a dear price in conflict, hostility, and resentment.

Temper Tirades

Everyone who has raised a toddler has probably been confronted at some point by a full-blown temper tantrum. Its fury is something to behold coming from a kid who only weighs twenty-five pounds. Usually a firm hand will discourage such violent behavior—but sometimes not. Some children throw tantrums specifically for the purpose of stirring up and manipulating the big powerful adults who claim to be in charge.

I knew one family, for example, that had a three-year-old boy who was still throwing the most terrible fits when he didn't get his way. He would fall on the floor—kick, scream, spit, and cry. His parents had done everything they knew to stop the tantrums, with no success. One night, they were reading the paper when the kid wanted them to do something. They didn't move quickly enough, so he went into his violent contortions. Out of exasperation, since the parents didn't know what else to do, they didn't do anything. They just went on reading. The child was shocked by their unresponsiveness. He got up, went over to his mother, shook her arm, and again fell screaming to the floor. Still neither parent reacted. He then approached his father and hit the newspaper before going into another tirade. By this point, Mom and Dad were secretly watching to see what would happen, but they remained passive. This kid felt so foolish and stupid throwing temper tantrums with no audience—that I never threw another one.

The next time your toddler goes a little crazy, you might try doing nothing. It worked in at least one case with which I am quite familiar.

DISCIPLINE

Challenge the Chief

Have you noticed that children will occasionally disobey their parents for the express purpose of testing just how much they can get away with? This game, called challenge-the-chief, can be played with surprising skill, even by very young children.

One father told me recently of taking his three-year-old daughter to a basketball game. Naturally, this kid was interested in everything in the gymnasium except the game, so the father permitted her to roam free. But first he walked her down to the stripe painted on the gym floor, and he told her not to go past that line. No sooner had he returned to his seat than she went scurrying down to that forbidden territory and stopped at the border. Then she flashed a grin at her father and deliberately put one foot over the line. It was as if she were saying, "Whatcha gonna do about it?"

Virtually every parent the world over has been asked that same question at one time or another. How it is answered is vitally important to the parent–child relationship. When a mom or dad ignores this kind of challenge, something changes in the mind of the child. For a particularly strong-willed boy or girl, that early test of parental leadership can grow into a full-blown case of rebellion during the troubled days of adolescence.

The ultimate paradox of childhood is that boys and girls want to be led by their parents, but they insist that their mothers and fathers earn the right to lead them. We should not miss the opportunity to do so.

Parental Authority

O ne writer on the subject of child development suggested that parents and children should be on an even playing field—making decisions by negotiation and compromise. After all, he said, who knows what is best for the boy or girl? Maybe the child is right and the parent is wrong.

When I heard that advice, with which I strongly disagree, I was reminded of a little hamster that once belonged to my daughter. One day I sat watching that furry little animal trying to get out of his cage. He worked tirelessly to open the gate and push his furry little nose between the bars. Then I noticed our dachshund, Siggie, sitting eight feet away in the shadows. He was watching the hamster, too. His ears were erect, and it was obvious what was on his mind. He was thinking, *Come on, baby. Open that door, and I'll have you for lunch.* If the hamster had been so unfortunate as to escape from his cage, which he desperately wanted to do, he would have been dead in a matter of seconds.

Obviously, I saw something from where I sat that the hamster couldn't have known. I had a different perspective than he did. I was aware of dangers that he couldn't have foreseen. That's why I denied him something that he desperately wanted to achieve.

So it is with children. Parents have the perspective of maturity that their kids lack. Sometimes the very thing they want most would be disastrous if they should be granted it. That's why I am a firm advocate of parental authority when children are young. Even though parents aren't perfect, most of them do what is best for their kids—and we must not undermine their ability to lead in their own homes.

This position is supported unequivocally by Scripture: The apostle Paul wrote, "Children, obey your parents in everything, for this pleases the Lord" (Colossians 3:20).

Shakespeare and Me

How do you teach basic honesty to kids? Well, I can tell you how my mother did it. When I was in the eighth grade, I was required to read some great books during the first semester. Like most fourteen-year-olds, however, I had other things on my mind.

I still hadn't begun the assignment as we approached the end of the term—so I selected the thickest, heaviest books in the library and told my teacher I had read them all. Consequently, she gave me an A+ on my report card. My mom was impressed, my dad was proud, and I was as guilty as sin.

In a moment of true confession, I admitted to my mother that I had cheated. Instead of getting mad at me or grounding me for six years, she simply said, quietly but with intensity, "Well, you'll just have to read the books."

"But, Mom," I said, "how can I read the collected works of William Shakespeare, *Ben Hur*, and about ten other huge books?"

"I don't know," she said, "but you're gonna do it." I spent the rest of that school year poring over the classics, while my friends played football and talked to girls outside my window. I'll tell you, it was grueling. No one ever paid more dearly for a little dishonesty. When the task was finally done, I went to my teacher and tearfully confessed the entire scam. She forgave me, and my mom let me rejoin the human race.

I never forgot that lesson in accountability, as painful as it was. But I'm glad the lady of the house didn't let me off the hook. She was too smart for that!

Mom Goes to School

I want to tell you about my mother, who was a master at trench warfare during my stubborn adolescent years. I could never hide anything from her for long, and she knew, intuitively, that I was getting into trouble at school.

One day she sat me down and said firmly, "I know you have been fooling around and giving your teachers a hard time. Well, I've thought it over, and I've decided that I'm not going to do anything about it. I'm not going to punish you. I'm not going to take away privileges. I'm not even going to talk about your foolishness anymore."

I was smiling until she added, "But I do want you to understand one thing. If the principal or the teachers ever call me, I promise you that the next day I'm going to school with you. I'll walk two feet behind you all day. I'll hold your hand in front of all your friends. When you sit in class, I'll climb into the seat with you. For one full day, you won't be able to shake me off."

That threat absolutely terrified me. It would have been social suicide to have my mother following me in front of my friends. No punishment would have been worse! Beat me, but don't go to school with me! I'm sure my teachers wondered why there was such a remarkable improvement in my behavior near the end of my freshman year in high school.

You might try my mom's approach with your teenagers. But please—don't tell them where you got the idea.

Linking Behavior to Consequences

Sheltering a child from the consequences of his or her behavior could help create an immature adult later.

One of the prime objectives during the preadolescent years is to teach a child that behavior leads inevitably to consequences. Unfortunately, that connection is often interrupted. For example, a seven-year-old begs for a dog but is never asked to feed and care for him. A ten-year-old is caught stealing candy from a store, but he's released to the custody of his parents. Nothing happens. A fifteen-year-old takes the keys to the family car, but the parents pay the fine for her driving without a license. So all through childhood, such loving parents, in their misguided efforts to shield the child from pain, have stood between his or her behavior and the natural consequences that flow from it. Under these circumstances, a young person may enter adulthood not really knowing that life can bite. He or she may become a grown-up adolescent constantly needing someone to bail him or her out of trouble.

How does one avoid this blunder? By linking behavior to consequences. If Jane carelessly loses her lunch money, she just may have to skip a meal. If Jack misses the school bus because he dawdled in the morning, he may have to walk to school.

Now obviously, it would be easy to carry this principle too far and become harsh. But a taste of bitter fruit that irresponsibility brings can teach a youngster valuable lessons that may be useful later on.

Using Reinforcement and Extinction

It's a well-known fact that behavior that is not rewarded will eventually disappear. This process is called "extinction," and it can be a very useful tool for parents and teachers.

Have you ever wondered, for example, why so many young children develop a tendency to whine when they speak to their parents? Simply stated, children whine because whining works. Mom and Dad are too busy and too preoccupied to respond to a normal voice. But they react immediately when their kids irritate them with a grating, unpleasant sound. What the parents are doing is rewarding (or "reinforcing") the whining response and extinguishing the more desirable behavior.

How can this process be reversed? Well, you might try saying, "Johnny, did you know I have very funny ears? They can't hear a whining voice. I can only hear a pleasant voice." Then proceed to ignore anything said in an irritating tone, but respond immediately when the normal voice is used. In this way, reward and extinction instantly become powerful tools for parents who understand properly how they work.

Remember this guiding principle: Behavior that produces desirable results will recur, and behavior that fails in the eyes of the child will tend to go away. It's as simple as that.

7

DIVORCE

A New Warning Label

In the 1960s, the surgeon general declared cigarettes harmful to the smoker's health. More recently, researchers have warned us about the dangers of foods high in fat and cholesterol. But we hear less about the health hazards of divorce.

Many studies have revealed the emotional and financial impact of divorce on couples and their children. But less well known is the research showing that divorce puts people at a high risk for psychiatric problems and physical disease.

Dr. David Larson, psychiatrist and researcher in Washington DC, reviewed medical studies on this subject and made some startling discoveries. For instance, being divorced and a nonsmoker is only slightly less dangerous than smoking a pack or more a day and staying married. Also, every type of terminal cancer strikes divorced individuals of both sexes more frequently than it does married people. What's more, premature death rates are significantly higher among divorced men and women. Physicians believe this is because the emotional trauma of divorce stresses the body and lowers the immune system's defense against disease.

In the light of this evidence, perhaps the surgeon general should consider warning married couples about the potential health risks of divorce. Certainly, healthy families are more beneficial to the well-being of children.

Strangers Marrying Strangers

Every year an astounding number of marriages disintegrate and leave deeply wounded people in their wake. But why is the casualty rate so high? One reason is the tendency for young men and women to marry virtual strangers. It's true that a typical couple talks for countless hours during the courtship period, and they believe they know each other intimately. But a dating relationship is designed to conceal information, not reveal it. Consequently, the bride and groom often enter into marriage with an array of private and conflicting opinions about how life's going to be lived after the wedding, and the stage is set for serious confrontations.

For this reason I strongly believe that each engaged couple should participate in at least six to eight sessions with a competent marriage counselor in order to identify the assumptions that each partner holds and to work through areas of potential conflict. When this occurs, some couples discover that they have unresolvable differences, and they agree to either postpone or call off the wedding. Others work through their conflicts and proceed toward marriage with increased confidence.

Either way, getting better acquainted before marriage is strategic. If by doing so we can reduce the tragedy of divorce by even 5 percent, it would certainly be worth the effort.

The Legacy of Divorce

How easily do children cope with the breakup of their family? The findings might surprise you.

California psychologist Judith Wallerstein is one of the most respected authorities on the effects of divorce. She has published numerous books and articles on this subject, including an investigation that should be brought to the attention of every parent. For twenty-five years, Wallerstein tracked hundreds of children of divorce, chronicling their lives from childhood through adolescence and adulthood. Her findings are discouraging.

Wallerstein found that the trauma experienced by young children after a divorce remains with them throughout their lives, making it more difficult to cope with challenges and difficulties. Adolescence and young adulthood are particularly stressful times. Later romantic relationships continue to be influenced by the memories of divorce.

In summary, Wallerstein said, "Unlike the adult experience, the child's suffering does not reach its peak at the breakup and then level off. The effect of the parents' divorce is played and replayed throughout the first three decades of the children's lives."[1]

If you and your spouse are getting a divorce, you should at least consider the consequences of that decision for the most vulnerable members of the family. The research shows that they will never be the same thereafter.

The Real Cost of Divorce

Divorce carries lifelong negative implications for children.

It's now known that emotional development in children is directly related to the presence of warm, nurturing, sustained, and continuous interaction with *both* parents. Anything that interferes with the vital relationship with either mother or father can have lasting consequences for the child.

One landmark study revealed that 90 percent of children from divorced homes suffered from an acute sense of shock when the separation occurred, including profound grieving and irrational fears.[2] Fifty percent reported feeling rejected and abandoned, and indeed half of the fathers never came to see their children three years after the divorce. One-third of the boys and girls feared abandonment by the remaining parent, and 66 percent experienced yearning for the absent parent with an intensity that researchers described as overwhelming. Most significantly, 37 percent of the children were even more unhappy and dissatisfied five years after the divorce than they had been at eighteen months. In other words, time did not heal their wounds.

That's the real meaning of divorce. It is certainly what I think about, with righteous indignation, when I see infidelity and marital deceit portrayed on television as some kind of exciting game for two. Some excitement. Some game.

Blended Families

I want to offer a word or two of advice to those who are planning to remarry after divorce or the death of a spouse. When children are involved, this is called a blended family, and it poses some very unique and unsettling challenges.

I can tell you that the Brady Bunch is a myth—the notion that a mom and dad with six kids can create one big happy family without conflict or rivalries. It just doesn't happen that way, although many blended families do eventually adjust to their new circumstances. Initially, at least, it is common within a blended family for one or more kids to see the new stepparent as a usurper. Their loyalty to the memory of their departed mother or father can be intense. For them to welcome a newcomer with open arms would be an act of betrayal. This places the stepparent in an impossible bind.

It is also common for one child to move into the power vacuum left by the departing parent. That youngster becomes the surrogate spouse. I'm not referring to sexual matters. Rather, that boy or girl begins relating to the remaining parent more as a peer. The status and power that come with that supportive role are very seductive, and a youngster can be unwilling to give them up.

These are only two of the land mines that can threaten blended families. Unfortunately there are others.

The Second Time Around

We've discussed blended families and the special challenges they typically face. But there is a more serious problem that can develop. It concerns the way the new husband and wife feel about their kids. Each is irrationally committed to his or her own flesh and blood, while being merely acquainted with the others. When fights and insults occur between the two sets of children, parents are almost always partial to those they brought into the world. It is natural for their allegiance to be directed to their own kids. Unfortunately, this creates a tendency for the blended family to dissolve into armed camps—us against them. If the kids sense this tension between parents, some will exploit it to gain power over siblings.

Some terrible battles can occur unless there are some ways to ventilate these feelings. Given the challenges, it is apparent why the probabilities of second and third marriages being successful are considerably lower than the first.

It is possible to blend families successfully, of course, and millions of people have done it. But the task *is* difficult, and you may need some help in pulling it off. That's why I strongly suggest that those planning to remarry seek professional counseling as early as possible. It is expensive, but another divorce is even more costly.

"But, Daddy…"

L et me share an actual letter written by a fourteen-year-old girl about her father.

> When I was ten, my parents got a divorce. Naturally, my father told me about it, 'cause he was my favorite.
>
> "Honey, I know it's been kind of bad for you these last few days, and I don't want to make it any worse, but there's something I have to tell you. Honey, your mother and I got a divorce."
>
> "But, Daddy…"
>
> "Now I know you don't want this, but it has to be done. Your mother and I just don't get along like we used to. I'm already packed, and my plane is leaving in half an hour."
>
> "But, Daddy, why do you have to leave?"
>
> "Well, honey, your mother and I just can't live together anymore."
>
> "Well, I know that, but I mean, why do you have to leave town?"
>
> "Oh, well, I've got someone waiting for me in New Jersey."
>
> "But, Daddy, will I ever see you again?"
>
> "Oh, sure you will, honey. We'll work something out."
>
> "OK, Daddy. Good-bye. Don't forget to write me."
>
> "I won't. 'Bye. Now, go to your room."
>
> "Daddy, I don't want you to go."
>
> "I know, honey, but I have to."
>
> "OK. Well, I guess that's the way life goes sometimes."
>
> After my father walked out that door, I never heard from him again.

The words written by that young girl need no elaboration. But she could tell you so much more!

8

EDUCATION AND LEARNING

Why We Study

It's been said that we forget more than 80 percent of what we learn. The obvious question is, why, then, should we go to the trouble of learning at all?

When you consider the cost of getting an education, it seems appropriate that we justify all that effort going into examinations, textbooks, homework, and countless hours spent in boring classrooms. Is education really worth what we invest in it?

In fact, it is. There are many valid reasons for learning, even if forgetting will take its usual toll. First, maybe the most important function of the learning process is the self-discipline and self-control that it fosters. Good students learn to follow directions, carry out assignments, and channel their mental faculties. Second, even if the facts and concepts can't be recalled, the individual knows they exist and where to find them. He or she can retrieve the information if needed. Third, old learning makes new learning easier. Each mental exercise gives us more associative cues with which to link future ideas and concepts, and we are changed for having been through the process of learning. Fourth, we don't really forget everything that is beyond the reach of our memories. The information is stored in the brain and will return to consciousness when properly stimulated. And fifth, we are shaped by the influence of intelligent and charismatic people who teach us.

I wish there were an easier, more efficient process for shaping human minds than the slow and painful experience of education. But until a learning pill is developed, the old-fashioned approach will have to do.

Learning to Write Right

Very few children learn to write adequately today, but it's a skill worth emphasizing at home.

The early development of my own writing career, which now includes more than twenty books, began when I was in elementary school. My parents encouraged me and helped me grow in this area. I remember writing a letter to a friend when I was nine years old. My mother then sat down with me and suggested that we read it together. I started the letter, "Dear Tom, how are you? I am just fine." My mom asked me if I thought that sounded a little boring. She said, "You haven't said anything. You used a few words, but they have no meaning." I never wrote that phrase again, although that is the typical way a child begins a letter.

Looking back, I can see how, even at an early age, my mother was teaching me to write. It's not terribly difficult or time-consuming to encourage kids and teach them some of the fundamentals. One approach is to ask a family member to correspond with your child and encourage him to write back. Then when your child shows you his reply, sprinkle a few corrections, like my mother offered, with a generous portion of praise. And then entice him to do a little creative expression.

It's also helpful to have a few English teachers who will invest themselves in a budding young writer. I had one in high school and another in college who were determined to teach me grammar and composition. They nearly beat me to death, but I earn a living today with the skills they gave me. Especially, I would like to say thanks to Dr. Ed Harwood. His classes were like marine boot camp, but what I learned there was priceless.

The ability to write has gone out of style—much like the old home-making classes for girls. But it is an incredibly valuable craft that your child can use in a wide variety of settings. Don't let him grow up without developing it.

Home Schooling

When our children were young, my wife and I were intent on giving them a good education. In those days we had only two options from which to choose: public schools or private schools. Today, there's a third alternative that warrants consideration.

The fastest-growing educational movement in the world today is the home-school phenomenon. More than 1.5 million U.S. parents and millions more in other countries have opted to teach their children at home—not for two or three years, but sometimes as long as twelve.[1] The movement is now old enough to allow for comparisons, and the results have been remarkable.

Universities and colleges are still enrolling their first big wave of home-schooled children, some of whom are the brightest and most well-adjusted students on campus. Standardized tests are verifying the efficiency of home-style learning. Some critics have worried about how home-schooled kids will be properly socialized, but here again the apprehension appears groundless. Almost every city now has a home-school association with activities and athletic leagues, orchestras, and organized field trips to bring the children together.

Admittedly, home schooling is not for everyone, but for those who are willing to pay the price, this third option is an idea whose time has come.

Myelinization

Have you ever wondered why an infant is unable to reach for an object or attempt to control the movement of his hands or feet? It's because the nervous system is inadequately insulated at birth. Electrical impulses are lost on their journey from the brain to other parts of the body. As the child grows, a whitish substance called myelin begins to coat the nerve fibers, allowing controlled muscular action to occur.

Myelinization typically proceeds from the head downward and from the center of the body outward. This is why a child can control the movement of his head and neck before the rest of the body, and the shoulder before the elbow, wrist, and fingers.

This understanding of myelin is important to the parents of boys, especially, who are slower to develop. Because a child's visual apparatus is among the last mechanism to be insulated, some immature boys and girls are unable to read, write, or spell until later. This helps explain why late bloomers often have early learning problems in school.[2]

Unfortunately, our culture permits few exceptions or deviations from the established educational timetable. Most six-year-olds start first grade whether they are ready or not. Some are not ready! Immature children should be home schooled or held out for a year. Most important, parents should be careful not to demand achievement from a child who is slow to develop. It may be physiologically impossible for him or her to match the successes of peers for a time, and that can be harmful.

Give myelinization a chance to do its work before challenging an undeveloped nervous system!

The Walleyed Pike

Let me tell you something interesting about the walleyed pike, which is a large fish with a prodigious appetite for minnows. Something surprising happens when a plate of glass is slipped into a tank of water, placing the pike on one side and the minnows on the other. The pike can't see the glass and solidly hits the barrier in pursuit of its dinner. Again and again it swims into the glass and bumps whatever one calls the front end of a walleye.

Eventually, the pike gives up. The fish apparently concludes that the minnows are not available. It will no longer try to catch them. At that point, the glass can be removed from the tank, allowing the minnows to swim around their mortal enemy in perfect safety. The pike will not molest them. It knows what it knows: They are unreachable. Amazingly, the walleyed pike will actually starve to death while surrounded by abundant amounts of food.[12]

This illustration is relevant not only to fish but in an interesting way to children. Just as a walleyed pike can become discouraged when faced with persistent failure, boys and girls react to it similarly. Early embarrassment or frustration in the classroom, such as an inability to read or spell, can have serious implications for kids. By the second or third year, some give up on school. Success is simply not available for them.

It is critical to obtain tutorial assistance for immature little kids who get off to a bad start. Early educational intervention may help them avoid giving up on "minnows" before it is too late.

Homework for Kids: Good or Bad?

How do you feel about homework being given during the elementary school years? Is it a good idea? And if so, how much is best?

Having written several books on discipline and being on record as an advocate of reasonable parental authority, my answer may surprise you: I believe homework for young children can be counterproductive if not handled very carefully. Little kids are asked to sit for five or more hours per day doing formal classwork. Many of them also take a tiring bus ride home. Then guess what? They're placed at a desk and told to do more assignments. For a wiry, active, fun-loving youngster, that's asking too much. Learning for them becomes an enormous bore instead of the exciting panorama that it ought to be.

Excessive homework during the early years also has the potential of interfering with family life. In our home we wanted our kids to participate in church activities, have some family time, and still be able to kick back and play after school. They needed to swing on the swings and play ball with their friends. Yet by the time their homework was done, darkness had fallen, dinnertime had arrived, baths were taken, and off they went to bed. Something just didn't feel quite right about that kind of pace.

Homework has a place in a child's education, but I think the time spent on after-school assignments in the early years should be very restricted. There are better things for the young to be doing after a long day in the classroom.

More Homework

L et me offer another word about homework assignments during the elementary school years. Though many educators and parents will disagree, I think time spent studying after school should be very limited.

In addition to the factors I mentioned, homework generates a considerable amount of stress for parents. Many kids either won't do the assignments, or they get tired and whine about them. That's when angry words begin to fly. I'm convinced that some frustrated parents lose their patience and subject their immature children to abusive situations.

When my wife, Shirley, was teaching second grade, one of her students came to school with both eyes black and swollen. The student reported that her father had beaten her because she couldn't learn her spelling words. That's illegal now, of course, but it was tragically tolerated in those days. That poor youngster will always think of herself as "stupid."

Then there are the parents who complete kids' assignments themselves just to get them over the hump. Have you ever worked for two weeks on a fifth-grade geography project for your eleven-year-old and then learned later that you got a C- on it? That's the ultimate humiliation.

In short, I believe homework in elementary school is appropriate for learning multiplication tables, spelling words, and test review. It's also helpful in training kids to bring home books, remember assignments, and complete them as required. But to burden them night after night with monotonous book work is to invite educational burnout. It is unwise to do that to an immature child!

Get 'Em Organized

What is the primary reason for failure in high school? The answer may surprise you.

According to educational consultant Cheri Fuller, the chief problem is not laziness or poor study skills. No, the main reason for poor school performance is disorganization. "Show me a student's notebook," Fuller says, "and I'll tell you whether that individual is a B student or a D student." An achieving student's notebook is arranged with dividers and folders for handouts and assignments. A failing student's notebook is usually a jumbled mess and may not even be used at all.

Some children are naturally sloppy, but most of them can learn to be better organized. Fuller says this skill should be taught during the elementary school years. Once they enter junior high, students may have as many as five teachers, each assigning different textbooks, workbooks, handouts, and assignments from various classroom subjects. It is foolish to assume that kids who have never had any organizational training will be able to keep such details straight and accessible. If we want them to function in this system, we need to give them the tools that are critical to success.

Organization! It's one very important key to success in school.

The Classic Underachiever

Have you ever seen those Bart Simpson T-shirts around? You know, the ones that say, "Underachiever—and Proud of It"? In real life, however, most underachievers are not really all that happy about their lack of performance.

The underachiever is a child who has the ability to do required schoolwork but does not have the self-discipline to perform. He slowly drives his mother, father, and teachers crazy as assignment after assignment hits the floor.

So what's a parent to do? Anger is the typical response, but it is most ineffective. Instead, I would make three recommendations that can reach some kids. First, since most underachievers are terribly disorganized, help establish a system for studying. Turn off the television set, and make sure the proper investment in homework is made. Second, stay in close contact with his teachers and know what's going on in school. I promise you that your underachieving son or daughter will *not* keep you so informed. And third, seek tutorial assistance to provide the one-on-one help that may make the difference.

Having offered that advice, however, let me speak now out of the other side of my mouth. There are some hard-core underachievers who seem determined to fail in school. For them no amount of pushing and shoving will get them motivated. In those cases I recommend that you go with the flow and accept the child just as he is. Not every youngster can be squeezed into the same mold, and it's a wise parent who knows when to race the engine and when to let it idle.

If there were a simple, single solution to the pervasive problem of underachievement, I'd put it in a bottle and sell it by the millions. It sure couldn't be any less helpful than those Bart Simpson T-shirts.

The Underachieving Child

We talked last time about the flighty, disorganized children who absolutely refuse to do assigned schoolwork. Let me share some additional thoughts about underachieving children.

First, these kids are not intrinsically inferior to their hardworking siblings. Yes, it would be wonderful if all students used their talents to best advantage. But children are unique individuals, and they don't have to fit the same mold. Besides, the classic underachievers sometimes outperform the academic superstars in the long run. That's what happened to Einstein, Edison, Eleanor Roosevelt, and others. So don't write off that disorganized, apparently lazy kid as a lifelong loser. He or she may surprise you.

Second, you will never turn an underachieving youngster into a scholar by nagging, pushing, threatening, and punishing. It just isn't in him. If you try to squeeze him into something he's not, you will only aggravate the child and frustrate yourself.

Third, stay as close as possible to the school. Your restless child isn't going to tell you what's going on there, so you need to find out for yourself. And seek tutorial assistance, if necessary, to keep him on track.

Fourth, your child lacks the discipline to structure his life. Help him generate it.

Finally, having done what you can to help, accept what he does in return. Go with the flow, and begin looking for other areas of success for your child. That advice will be best for your son or daughter and, I assure you, much easier on your nerves, too!

Who's at Fault?

I want to say a word or two today on behalf of the public schools, and especially to the men and women who serve our children there.

First, let me acknowledge that I share the concern of many others about falling test scores, increasing violence on campuses, and the high illiteracy rate. On the other hand, it is not fair to blame educators for all that has gone wrong. The teachers and school administrators who guide our children have been among the most maligned and underappreciated people in our society. It's a bum rap.

We would still be having serious difficulties in our schools if the professionals did everything right. Why? Because what goes on in the classroom can't be separated from the problems occurring in the culture at large. Educators aren't responsible for the condition of our kids when they arrive at school each morning. It's not the teachers' fault that families are unraveling and that large numbers of their students have been abused, neglected, and undernourished. They can't keep kids from watching mindless television or violent videos until midnight or from using illegal substances and alcohol. In essence, when the culture begins to crumble, the schools will also look bad.

Even though I disagree with some of the trends in modern education, I sympathize with the dedicated teachers and principals out there who are doing their best on behalf of our youngsters. They're a discouraged lot today, and they need our support.

9

EMOTIONS

Cradles of Eminence

It is well known that a difficult childhood leaves some people wounded and disadvantaged for the rest of their lives. But for others, early hardships actually fuel great achievement and success. The difference appears to be a function of individual temperaments and resourcefulness.

In a classic study called *Cradles of Eminence,* Victor and Mildred Goertzel investigated the home backgrounds of three hundred highly successful people. The researchers sought to identify the early experiences that may have contributed to remarkable achievement. All of the subjects were well known for their accomplishments; they included Einstein, Freud, Churchill, and many others.[1]

The backgrounds of these people proved very interesting. Three-fourths of them came from troubled childhoods, enduring poverty, broken homes, or parental abuse. One-fourth had physical handicaps. Most of those who became writers and playwrights had watched their own parents embroiled in psychological dramas of one sort or another. The researchers concluded that the need to compensate for disadvantages was a major factor in the drive toward personal achievement.

The application to your own family should be obvious. If your child has gone through a traumatic experience or is physically disadvantaged, don't give up hope. Help identify his or her strengths and natural abilities that can be used to overcome the handicap.

Whether your child's challenges ultimately weaken or strengthen him or her may be influenced by the way you respond to the crisis. The problem that seems so formidable today may become the inspiration for greatness tomorrow.

Engine and Caboose

Did you hear the one about the wedding ceremony where the minister said, "Do you take this woman for better or for worse? For richer or for poorer? In sickness and in health?" And the groom said, "Yes, no, yes, no, no, yes."

Of course, we'd all like to sign up for the better, richer, and healthier parts when we get married and forget all that other stuff. But that's not the way marriage works because that's not the way life works.

I heard of another wedding ceremony, this one real, during which the bride and groom pledged to stay married as long as they continued to love each other. Well, I hope they both know good divorce attorneys, because they're going to need them. Relationships based on feelings are necessarily ephemeral and transitory. The only real stability in marriage is produced by firm commitments that hold two people steady when emotions are fluctuating wildly. Without this determination to cement human relationships, they are destined to disintegrate.

Can you imagine a parent saying to the child, "I'll care for you for as long as I shall love you"? That would hardly portend stability and well-being for the child. Nor does a wishy-washy expression of love hold much promise for the future of a marriage.

Emotion might be thought of as the caboose on a train. A committed will is the engine that pulls the relationship through all the ups and downs of everyday living.

Depressed Children

We used to believe that only adults suffered from depression, but that understanding is changing. Now we're seeing signs of serious despondency in children as young as five years old.

Symptoms of depression in an elementary schoolchild may include general lethargy, a lack of interest in things that used to excite him or her, sleep disturbances, chewed fingernails, loss of appetite, and violent emotional outbursts. Stomach complaints can be another tip-off, as well as intolerance to frustration.

If you suspect that your child is beginning to show the signs of depression, you should help him or her verbalize feelings. Try to anticipate the explanation for sadness or anger, and lead the youngster into conversations that provide an opportunity to ventilate. Make yourself available to listen without judging or belittling the feelings expressed. Simply being understood is soothing for children and adults alike.

If the problem persists, I urge you to seek professional help. Prolonged depression can be destructive for human beings of any age, and it is especially dangerous to children.

Dishonest Emotions

I had a friend who won a Bronze Star for courage in Vietnam. But the first night his unit arrived on the battlefield, he and the other men were scared to death. They dug foxholes and nervously watched the sun disappear beyond the horizon. At approximately midnight, the enemy attacked with a vengeance. Before long, all the soldiers were firing frantically and throwing hand grenades in the darkness. The battle raged throughout the night, and the troops appeared to be winning. At last the sun came up, and the body count began. But not one dead Vietcong soldier lay at the perimeter of the mountain. In fact, no enemy had ever been there. The nervous troops had imagined the entire attack.

The reaction of the men was typical of frightened people of any age. The mind will generate evidence to validate anxieties. A person who fears cancer, for example, will sometimes develop all the telltale symptoms even though no disease process is there. And a child who awakens at night will "hear" scary sounds echoing through the house. That's just the way our emotions work. So before you panic, cool down a bit. The danger might be, and probably is, imaginary.

Inveterate Liars

We've been discussing the nature of human emotions and how they distort reality. Here's another example:

The city of Los Angeles was paralyzed with fear in 1969 when Charles Manson and his "family" murdered many people in cold blood. Residents wondered who would be next. My mother was quite convinced that she was the prime candidate. Sure enough, Mom and Dad heard the intruder as they lay in bed one night.

Thump came the sound from the area of the kitchen.

"Did you hear that?" asked my mother.

"Yes, be quiet," said my father.

They lay staring into the darkness, breathing shallowly and listening for further clues. A second *thump* brought them to their feet. They felt their way to the bedroom door, which was closed. Mom propped her foot against the door and threw her weight against the upper section. My father characteristically wanted to confront the attacker head-on. He reached through the darkness and grasped the doorknob, but his pull met the resistance from my mother. Dad assumed someone was holding the door from the other side, while my mother could feel the killer trying to force it open.

My parents stood there in the blackness, struggling against one another and imagining themselves to be in a tug-of-war with a killer. Finally Mother ran to the window to scream, which allowed Dad to open the door. That's when she noticed that the light was on in the hall. In reality, no prowler was there. The thumps were never identified, and Charles Manson never made his anticipated visit.

This story illustrates the way fearful people can be deceived by human emotions. Feelings are inveterate liars that often confirm our worst fears.

That's why I wrote a book whose title asked this question, Emotions: Can you trust them? It took me two hundred pages to say no!

Terrors by Night

Have you ever been awakened in the middle of the night by a boy or girl who was obviously terrified but couldn't explain why? That child may have just experienced what is known as a night terror—which is very different from a nightmare. It's important to understand the difference.

If children are awakened in the midst of a nightmare, they can usually describe the "story" and tell you what was so scary about it. Then they can be comforted and tucked in for the rest of the night. But youngsters in the midst of night terrors usually can't be brought to consciousness, even though they may sit up in bed with eyes open, screaming and shaking pitifully. It's as if they're in another world that won't even be remembered the next morning.

It appears that night terrors occur in what is known as stage-four sleep, which is deeper and further from consciousness than any other human experience. In this state, the body's mechanisms are reduced to a bare minimum to sustain life. Breathing, heart rate, metabolism, and other functions go into superslow motion. Nightmares, on the other hand, occur in stage-three sleep, which means they're closer to consciousness and are linked to events in one's waking life.

The good news is that there appear to be no physical or psychological problems associated with night terrors. You can, in fact, prevent them with a mild dose of medication. However, most physicians don't recommend doing so unless they're disturbing the parents' stage-four sleep.

Night terrors and nightmares. It's a distinction worth remembering.

The Earthquake

We discussed previously a phenomenon known as night terrors, those frightening experiences that some children have while sleeping and that are very different from nightmares.

My own daughter had such an experience when she was four years old. About midnight one night, she began screaming from her bed. When I reached her side, she was babbling excitedly about the fact that the wall was about to fall on her.

She was saying, "Daddy, it's falling, it's falling. The wall is falling!" even though she wasn't awake.

I pressed the child's hand against the wall and said, "Honey, that wall has been there a long time. It's very strong. It isn't going to fall. You are OK. Go back to sleep. Everything is all right."

I don't believe Danae ever came to consciousness. I tucked her under the covers and went back to sleep myself. Six hours later, on the morning of February 9, 1971, a powerful 6.1 earthquake rattled the city of Los Angeles and shook my wife and me out of bed. I rushed to Danae's room to get her out of the way of that wall, which was violently jumping and shaking above her bed.

Did our four-year-old have some kind of forewarning of the earthquake in the midnight hours? I don't know, but I'll tell you this: The next time she tells me the wall is going to fall, I intend to believe her!

FATHERHOOD

Fathers and Daughters

Long before a teenage girl finds her first real boyfriend or falls in love, her attitude toward men has been shaped by her father. Why? Because the father–daughter relationship sets the stage for all future romantic involvement.

If a young woman's father is an alcoholic and a bum, she'll spend her life trying to find a man who can meet the needs her father never fulfilled in her heart. If he's warm and nurturing, she'll look for a lover to equal him. If he thinks she's beautiful and feminine, she'll be inclined to see herself that way. But if he rejects her as unattractive and uninteresting, she's likely to carry self-image problems into her adult years.

I've also observed that a woman's relationship with her future husband is significantly influenced by the way she perceived her father's authority. If he was overbearing or capricious during her earlier years, she may be inclined to precipitate power struggles with her husband throughout married life. But if Dad blended love and discipline in a way that conveyed strength, she may be more comfortable with a give-and-take marriage characterized by mutual respect.

So much of what goes into marriage starts with a girl's father. That's why it behooves us as dads to give our best effort to the raising of those kids around our feet.

A Good Man, Who Can Find?

R emember when *pot* was something you cooked in and *bad* really
meant bad, not good?

It's strange how some words pass in and out of common usage. David
Blankenhorn, the head of an organization that studies cultural values,
points out that the compliment "good family man" is one of the phrases
that has gone into obscurity.[1] It was once widely used in our culture to
designate a true badge of honor. The rough translation would be, "someone who puts his family first."

Look at the three words that make up that phrase. *Good* refers to
widely accepted moral values. *Family* points to purposes larger than the
self. And *man* says there's a norm of masculinity. It seems that contempo-
rary culture no longer celebrates a widely shared ideal of such a man who
puts his family first.

Where do we see responsible masculinity represented on television?
Bill Cosby modeled it for a few years, but who else has been portrayed in
the media as a good family man? There just aren't many. No, we're more
likely to hear about superstar athletes or the ladies' man or the entrepre-
neur who's sacrificed all, including his wife and children, to make his start-
up company a success.

Fortunately, it's not too late to bring this simple phrase back into
vogue. "A good family man." It is indeed one of the highest callings to
which a man can aspire.

Fathers and the Empty Nest

When we hear the phrase "empty nest" we often think of mothers who are going through pain and depression as their children move away. But research shows that fathers feel the pain as well—in many cases even more intensely than their wives.

The movie *Father of the Bride* is hilarious. But it's also a touching tribute to the love of a father for his daughter. When George, the dad, sits across from his daughter at the dinner table and learns that she's engaged, he takes the news hard. He can't believe what he's hearing. He has to clear his vision as he sees her as a little baby girl, and then as the tomboy of eight or ten years, and finally as a beautiful young woman of eighteen. His little girl has grown up, and she's leaving him. He will never again be the main man in the life of this baby or this little girl or this beautiful young adult. A part of his life is over, and there's grieving to be done.

George's experience is not so unusual. A recent study asked four hundred parents of college freshmen to report their feelings when their son or daughter left home. Surprisingly to some, the fathers took it harder than the mothers. And one of the chief explanations was regret. Fathers had been so busy—working so hard—that they suddenly realized it was too late to build a relationship with the then-grown child.

If you still have teenagers at home, take a moment regularly to enjoy your remaining time together. Those days will be gone in the blink of an eye.

Tim and Christine Burke

Would you be willing to give up your career, your aspirations, and a $600,000 annual salary if your family was in need? I know a man who did.

In 1985 Tim Burke saw his boyhood dream come true the day he was signed to pitch for the Montreal Expos. After four years in the minors, he was finally given a chance to play in the big leagues. And he quickly proved to be worth his salt—setting a record for the most relief appearances by a rookie player.

Along the way, however, Tim and his wife, Christine, adopted four children with very special needs—two daughters from South Korea, a handicapped son from Guatemala, and another son from Vietnam. All of the children were born with very serious illnesses or defects. Neither Tim nor Christine was prepared for the tremendous demands such a family would bring. And with the grueling schedule of major-league baseball, Tim was seldom around to help. So in 1993, only three months after signing a $600,000 contract with the Cincinnati Reds, he decided to retire.

When pressed by reporters to explain this unbelievable decision, he simply said, "Baseball is going to do just fine without me. But I'm the only father my children have."

Heroes are in short supply these days. Tim and Christine Burke are two of them.

A Great Father

Someone has said, "Link a boy to the right man, and he will seldom go wrong." That adage is even truer when the "right man" happens to be his dad.

The influence of a good father is incalculable, reverberating for generations and shaping the character of his children. I was blessed to have had that kind of dad. He was a wonderful man—not because of his accomplishments or successes. He was great because of the way he lived his life, his devotion to Jesus Christ, and the love he expressed for his family.

My father has been gone since 1977, and I miss him still. I'll never forget the telephone call I received from a minister saying that my dad had suffered a massive heart attack and wasn't expected to live through the night. As I flew to Kansas City, I thought about the memorable times we spent together and the very happiest moments of my childhood.

We would get up very early on a wintry morning, put on our hunting clothes, and head twenty miles out of town to our favorite place. We'd climb over the fence and follow a little creek for several miles leading to an area that I called "the big woods"—because the trees looked so huge to me. Dad would get me situated under a fallen tree that made a secret room, and then we'd wait for the sun to rise. The entire panorama of nature would unfold out there in the woods as the squirrels, chipmunks, and birds awakened before us. Those moments together with my dad were priceless to me. Conversations occurred out there that didn't happen anywhere else. How could I have gotten very angry at a dad who took the time to be with me? The interactions we shared in that setting made me want to be like that man—to adopt his values as my values, his dreams as my dreams, and his God as my God. His pervasive influence continues in my life today.

That's the power of a man to set a kid on the right road. I can think of no wiser investment in the entire realm of human experience.

Of Elephants and Teenagers

Other than dogs, which I have always loved, the animals that fascinate me most are elephants. These magnificent creatures are highly intelligent and have very complex emotional natures. I suppose that's what makes it disturbing when we see them suffering the encroachment of civilization.

That is happening in the Pilanesberg National Park in northwestern South Africa. Rangers there have reported that young bull elephants in that region have become increasingly violent in recent years—especially to nearby white rhinos. Without provocation, they knock them over and then kneel and gore them to death. This is not typical elephant behavior, and it has been very difficult to explain.

But now game wardens think they've cracked the code. Apparently, the aggressiveness is a by-product of government programs to reduce elephant populations by killing the older animals. Almost all of the young rogues were orphaned when they were calves, depriving them of adult contact. Under normal circumstances, dominant older males keep the young bulls in line and serve as role models for them. In the absence of that influence, juvenile delinquents grow up to terrorize their neighbors.[2]

Now, I know it's risky to apply animal behavior too liberally to human beings, but the parallel here is too striking to miss. Thirty percent of all American children were born out of wedlock, and in the African-American community, the number is above 70 percent.[3] Most of these kids grow up without masculine role models and discipline. The result is often catastrophic—for teenagers *and* for elephants.

MacArthur

The year was 1962, and General Douglas MacArthur was by then an old and feeble man. He had been one of the greatest military heroes of all time, leading our armies in World Wars I and II and in Korea. By then his better days were behind.

MacArthur had returned that day to his beloved West Point, where he had been a cadet some sixty years before. He had come that day to say good-bye. His speech on the Plain that day was one of the most powerful ever given. It was entitled "Duty, Honor, Country" and ended with these words:

> The shadows are lengthening for me. The twilight is here. My days of old have vanished—tone and tints. They have gone glimmering through the dreams of things that were. Their memory is of wondrous beauty, watered by tears and coaxed and caressed by the smiles of yesterday. I listen, then, but with thirsty ear, for the witching melody of faint bugles blowing Reveille, of far drums beating the long roll.
>
> In my dreams I hear again the crash of guns, the rattle of musketry, the strange mournful mutter of the battlefield. But in the evening of my memory, I come back to West Point. Always there echoes and re-echoes, "Duty, Honor, Country." Today marks my final roll call with you, but I want you to know that when I cross the river, my last conscious thoughts will be of the Corps, and the Corps, and the Corps. I bid you farewell.[4]

General Douglas MacArthur died less than two years later on April 5, 1964. It seems fitting that we who enjoy the sweet benefits of freedom pause to thank the general and millions of others in uniform who died in the defense of liberty. We owe them an enormous debt. They lived by a code of "Duty, Honor, Country"!

11

GETTING OLDER

Your Birthday

Do fall and springtime frighten you?
My father was an artist and a poet—not by profession only but also by the beating of his heart—by the very soul of his being. When my mother turned fifty years of age, Dad naturally saw the significance of that milestone and recognized within it the passing of the years and the brevity of life. It inspired him to write a poem that he called "Your Birthday." These are his words:

> The whole world is singing, now that Spring has come.
> I saw a robin in the morning sun.
> Among the pale green leaves and bursting buds,
>   I heard his talk.
> But it is Autumn, where we walk.
>
> 'Tis true for us, the Summer too is gone.
> Now, whiplash winds arise, and further on
> The ice and sleet and cold in grim assault
>   to pierce us through.
> Does fall and springtime frighten you?
>
> Impotent shines the April sun so fair,
> To melt the wisps of frost within your hair
> My dear, I know you feel the threatening gloom—
>   but I'm with you
> And hand in hand, we'll face the Winter too.

Well, my mother and father did face the winter together. Now they lie side by side on a windswept hill where they once loved to wait. And now my wife and I are experiencing "fall and springtime."

It's Never Too Late

The world seems to worship youth and is terrified of aging. But there was a time when getting older was associated with wisdom and experience. In fact, some of the greatest accomplishments in history came very late in life.

Immanuel Kant wrote one of his best philosophical works at the age of seventy-four. Verdi penned his classic "Ave Maria" at eighty-five. Alfred, Lord Tennyson was eighty when he wrote "Crossing the Bar." Michelangelo was eighty-seven when he completed *The Pietà*, his greatest work of art. Justice Oliver Wendell Holmes set down some of his most brilliant opinions at the age of ninety. Titian painted his famous *Allegory of the Battle of Lepanto* at the age of ninety-eight. And Ronald Reagan was the most powerful man in the world at seventy-five.[1]

Generally speaking, older people today are healthier than ever before, and anything that squanders their talents is foolish. While we're on the subject, it irritates me that television advertisers are only interested in programming for the younger set. Isn't a tube of toothpaste sold to an eighty-year-old just as profitable as one pitched to a kid?

This notion that life should be winding down at fifty or sixty years of age is crazy. If you're a baby boomer, I'll bet you agree with me. Let's not limp off the stage before we absolutely must.

Talking Scale

A few years ago, my staff bought me a "talking scale" for my birthday. I never told them how badly I hated that thing. It had no volume control and shouted my weight all over the neighborhood. Nevertheless, I went on a two-week diet shortly thereafter and used the scale to monitor my weight loss. Every morning I would get out of bed and climb on board, to which a man's voice would respond by giving me the good (or bad) news.

About twelve days later I hopped on the scale one morning, and it promptly told me I weighed 278 pounds. I couldn't have gained eighty pounds in one day, so I got off and back on again. This time it said, "Your weight is 147 pounds." Every time I stepped on the scale, it reported a different number. Why had it suddenly gone bonkers?

Finally, I stepped up again, and the crazy thing didn't say anything. I stood there in my pajamas, feeling stupid and waiting for this cuckoo machine to talk to me. After a long pause, a very tired voice said, "Myyyyyy baaatterreez aaarrrrrrr loooooooow."

I said, "I know, buddy. So are mine."

You may be suffering today from that chronic illness known as "low batteries." The best cure for a power failure is a radical change of pace— even if it's only for a day or two. Take off. Get out. Play hooky. Go shopping. Do something that you've been wanting to do, just for fun.

Then, perhaps, you'll come home with your batteries recharged and raring to go.

Four on Four

I've always loved the game of basketball, even though I've never been particularly skilled at it. But a few years ago, at age fifty, I had the opportunity of a lifetime. My friends and I had gone to a conference in Laguna, California, which is a beach town populated mostly by surfers and sun worshipers. During an afternoon break, someone suggested that four of us old guys go down to the outdoor basketball court on the beach and challenge the young hotshots who play there. It was a stupid thing to do, but off we went.

When we arrived, about three hundred spectators surrounded the court, where four-man teams waited to take their turn against the reigning champs. We got in the line waiting to play. Rumors began to spread about who these old dudes really were. Some thought we were NBA scouts checking out the talent. Others thought we were coaches from USC or UCLA. Why else would we be there! As for me, I've never been so nervous in my life as I was while waiting to play the champs.

We finally stepped onto the court, and the impossible happened. We got hot and hit everything we shot. Within two minutes, we were ahead by a score of eight to nothing. The crowd went crazy as people began to come from everywhere on the beach. Only three more buckets and we would have pulled off the upset of the century. But then reality set in, and we lost eleven to eight.

Alas, athletic immortality often hangs by the slenderest thread. I missed it by three lousy buckets. How close have you come?

The Last Leaf on the Tree

Let me share a classic poem about old age entitled "The Last Leaf on the Tree." It is a favorite of mine written by Oliver Wendell Holmes.

> I saw him once before as he passed by the door and again.
> The pavement stones resound as he toddles
>   o'er the ground with his cane.
>
> They say that in his prime, e'er the pruning knife
>   of time cut him down,
> not a better man was found by the crier on his
>   round through the town.
>
> But now he walks the streets and he looks at
>   all he meets, sad and wan.
> And he shakes his feeble head and it seems as if
>   he said, "They're gone."
>
> My grandmama has said, poor old lady,
>   she is dead long ago,
> that he had a Roman nose and his cheek
>   was like a rose in the snow.
>
> But now his nose is thin, and it rests upon
>   his chin like a staff.
> And a crook is in his back and a melancholy
>   crack is in his laugh.
>
> I know it's a sin, for me to sit and grin at him here,
> but the old three-cornered hat and the britches
>   and all that are so queer.
>
> And if I should live to be the last leaf
>   on the tree in the spring,
> let them smile as I do now at the old
>   forsaken bough, where I cling.

Is there a last leaf on the tree somewhere who needs a little encouragement from you today? Why not give him or her a call?

Grandma's off Her Rocker

There was a time when uncles, aunts, brothers, and sisters were available to give parents a helping hand with child rearing. But more typically today, the extended family is spread all over the continent and might not be trusted anyway. Even grandparents are sometimes unavailable because they're just as busy as their kids. Let me share a humorous poem that describes this situation. I have no idea who wrote this little piece, but I think you'll enjoy it. It's called "Where Have All the Grandmas Gone?"

> In the dim and distant past,
> When life's tempo wasn't fast,
> Grandma used to rock and knit,
> Crochet, tat, and babysit.
>
> When the kids were in a jam,
> They could always call on "Gram."
> In that day of gracious living,
> Grandma was the gal for giving.
>
> But today she's in the gym,
> Exercising to keep slim.
> She's off touring with the bunch,
> Or taking clients out to lunch.
>
> Going north to ski or curl,
> All her days are in a whirl.
> Nothing seems to stop or block her,
> Now that Grandma's off her rocker![2]

Well, now we know why Grandma isn't at home waiting for a call. I think it's wonderful that older people are busy and productive. But if that means they don't have time for grandkids, we're all the losers for it. Children need not only mothers and fathers who are dedicated to them but also older adults who are invested in their lives. The people most qualified to fulfill that responsibility are loving grandmas and grandpas who are passionately committed to their own flesh and blood.

12

GRACE AND FORGIVENESS

A Great Cup of Tea

Have you noticed that children sometimes try to be helpful, but it only makes your life more complicated?

I heard a story about a mother who was sick in bed with the flu. Her darling daughter wanted so much to be a good nurse. She fluffed the pillows and brought a magazine for her mother to read. And then she even showed up with a surprise cup of tea.

"Why, you're such a sweetheart," the mother said as she drank the tea. "I didn't know you even knew how to make tea."

"Oh, yes," the little girl replied. "I learned by watching you. I put the tea leaves in the pan and then I put in the water, and I boiled it, and then I strained it into a cup. But I couldn't find a strainer, so I used the flyswatter instead."

"You what?" the mother screamed.

And the little girl said, "Oh, don't worry, Mom, I didn't use the new flyswatter. I used the old one."

When kids try their hardest and they get it all wrong in spite of themselves, what's a parent to do? What mothers and fathers often do is prevent their children from carrying any responsibility that could result in a mess or a mistake. It's just easier to do everything for them than to clean up afterward. But I urge parents not to fall into that trap.

Your child needs his mistakes. That's how he learns. So go along with the game every now and then...even if the tea you drink tastes a little strange.

You Always Bite the One You Love

Isn't it curious how in the midst of a nasty family argument we can shake out of the bad mood the instant the telephone rings or a neighbor knocks on the door?

Sometimes those we love are treated the worst, and kids are quick to notice this hypocrisy. Have you ever been brought up short by a small voice questioning this sudden turn to peaches and cream after twenty minutes of fire and brimstone?

The late Mark Hatfield, a longtime senator from Oregon and the father of four kids, said his wife stung him once by saying, "I just wish you were as patient with your children as you are with your constituents."

He isn't alone. We're all guilty at times of what I call "split vision," treating certain people with forbearance while heaping contempt on others under our own roof. We assume the worst; we pounce on every shortcoming. We never miss an opportunity to deliver a corrective harangue. And in the process, we wound the people we care about the most.

Isn't it time to cut one another a little slack at home? If, in fact, we love our spouses and our children and our parents as much as we say we do, one way to show it is to give them the kind words we bestow on our casual acquaintances.

The Only Cure for Bitterness

Have you noticed how difficult it is to forgive those who have wronged us? It's even harder when the offenders are our parents.

When we are young, our emotions are so intense that any wounds and injuries may stay with us for a lifetime. The pain is immeasurably worse when the one who wronged us was a parent. Perhaps a mother rejected us instead of providing the love we needed. Maybe an alcoholic father was sexually abusive in the midnight hours. Little victims of such horror may still be consumed by resentment and anger many decades later.

Psychologists and ministers now agree that there is only one cure for the cancer of bitterness. It is to forgive, which Dr. Archibald Hart defines as "giving up my right to hurt you for hurting me."[1] Only when we find the emotional maturity to release those who have wronged us, whether they have repented or not, will the wounds finally start to heal.

Jesus said it like this: "And when you stand praying, if you hold anything against anyone, forgive them, so that your Father in heaven may forgive you your sins" (Mark 11:25). Note that Jesus said nothing about who was right and who was wrong. Forgiveness, like love, must be unmerited and unconditional. Forgiveness begins the healing process.

Love Is Having to Say "I'm Sorry"

Many people have a hard time saying that they're sorry to anyone, let alone to their children, but there are times when it's the only thing to do. Apologizing when we're wrong provides opportunities to teach valuable lessons to our sons and daughters.

I remember one evening after a very hard day of work when I was especially grouchy with my ten-year-old daughter. After going to bed that night, I just felt like I hadn't treated her right and that I needed to ask her for forgiveness. So before she left for school the next morning, I said, "Honey, I know that you know that daddies aren't perfect, and I have to admit that I wasn't fair with you last night. I want you to forgive me." She put her arms around my neck, and she shocked me down to my toes. She said, "I knew you were gonna have to say that, Daddy, and it's OK. I forgive you."

Like my daughter, most children are very resilient, and they're eager to reconcile. Although you may have to sputter out the words, asking a child for forgiveness when you're wrong shows that you have flaws and imperfections like everyone else. And it models apologetic behavior for them.

In the family where no apologies are offered, problems are often swept under the rug. But by saying "I'm sorry" you can bring a world of healing and calm to an irritable and stressed-out household. It's a humbling experience, to be sure, but we can all stand a little unscheduled humility.

Forgiveness in Paducah

You probably remember the tragedy in the small town of Paducah, Kentucky. A fourteen-year-old boy named Michael Carneal opened fire on a group of students who had gathered in prayer. Within seconds, ten of them had been wounded, three of them fatally.

Who is this Michael Carneal, and what do we know about his earlier years? Well, he wasn't into drugs, crime, or cults. He was a solid B student who seldom got into trouble—either in school or at home. Still, there were signs. The theme of his school essays revealed that he felt "small and powerless." Friends say he was always angry about being teased in school. That has become a familiar pattern among those who commit acts of unprovoked violence.

While we need to understand more about Michael, I'm more interested in the other young men and women of Paducah. These kids showed a remarkable willingness to forgive. Placards began appearing at the high school, reading, We Forgive You, Mike. Kelly Carneal, Michael's sister, was not only embraced by her peers but also asked to sing in the choir at the slain girls' funeral. And during the town's annual Christmas parade, a moment of silent prayer was lifted up on behalf of Michael and his family.

One young girl said it best: "I can hate Michael and bear the scars of what he did for the rest of my life. But I choose to forgive him and get beyond it."[2]

What impressive maturity from teenagers under fire.

13

HEALTH AND SAFETY

Keeping the Brain Healthy

Did you hear about the ninety-four-year-old man who went to the doctor because his hip was aching? The doctor examined him and said, "Well, what do you expect? You're ninety-four years old!" The man replied, "Well, how come my other hip doesn't know that?"

Is it possible to grow old without parts of our body—especially our brain—wearing out? Specifically, are there techniques for remaining mentally alert as we age? An article in *Family Circle* magazine suggested five ways to maintain healthy minds through the aging process.[1] The first rule is to "use it or lose it." The human brain isn't like a calculator that you can plug in and leave idle for a year and find working just as well when you return. It must have constant use and regular input of sensory information.

Second, proper brain function is dependent on a balanced diet with ample supplies of all the essential nutrients.

Third is exercise. Every organ of the body, including the package of neural matter with which we think, benefits from physical activity.

Fourth is regular physical examinations and good health care. Untreated disease processes can affect us physically and mentally.

Finally, the fifth way to keep our brains healthy is by having an active social life. Being sick, isolated, and alone is a prescription for rapid mental decline.

Unfortunately, many older citizens are unable to implement these five suggestions for one reason or another. Some are alone and have no one to talk to. Others lack the resources for good medical care and healthy nutrition.

That's why those of us in the younger generation owe today's seniors our time and attention. They cared for us when we were frail and helpless. Now it's our time to return the favor.

Infant Mortality

Peter Brimelow, writing in a recent issue of *Forbes*, described the terrible curse of maternal and infant mortality during the eighteenth and nineteenth centuries. Death in that era came calling at nearly every door, whether humble or proud. In the 1700s one baby in five died in infancy, and thirty-three mothers out of every one thousand were lost in childbirth. Abraham Lincoln suffered the loss of a child in infancy, and a well-known minister, Cotton Mather, buried eight of his children before their second birthdays.

As for the deaths of mothers in that era, it may be difficult for us to understand today just what that meant to the families, but it was usually devastating. It wasn't uncommon for a woman with eight or ten children to die during yet another delivery, leaving a grief-stricken father to raise his kids while continuing the exhausting tasks of farming or ranching. The rate of infant and maternal mortality remained terribly high well into the modern era. Given this history, we have much to be thankful for today. The current death rate for mothers in childbirth is only one in 14,285 and for babies only one in 1,400.[2]

It is appropriate that we pause today to acknowledge the remarkable achievements of medical science and to tip our hats to the men and women who continue to make pregnancy and childbirth a relatively safe experience.

Fetal Alcohol Syndrome

Fetal alcohol syndrome is a condition occurring in babies and children whose mothers indulged in alcoholic beverages during pregnancy. Unfortunately, damage can occur throughout the entire nine months of gestation, but it is especially damaging during the first trimester of development. Alcohol in the blood of the mother at that time can produce devastating problems, including heart anomalies, central nervous system dysfunction, head and facial abnormalities, and lifelong behavior problems. And tragically, fetal alcohol syndrome is thought to be the leading cause of mental retardation.[3]

There is a dramatic reference to alcohol and pregnancy in the Old Testament. You may remember the story of Samson, who terrorized his enemies, the Philistines, with enormous feats of strength. Before Samson was born, his mother was told by an angel that her child was destined for greatness and that she must not weaken him by imbibing strong drink while she was pregnant.[4] As it turns out, the angel knew what he was talking about! Medical science has now verified the wisdom of that advice. That's why a warning to pregnant women is posted, by law, wherever liquor, beer, and wine are sold.

If you're pregnant, or you anticipate becoming pregnant, don't take chances with your baby's future. There is no level of alcohol that is known to be safe. Abstain for the entire nine months. You and your baby will be so glad you did.

The Ultimate Child Abuse

Today's extreme emphasis on physical attractiveness and body consciousness is harmful to adults—and potentially life-threatening to children.

A study done at the University of California has shown that 80 percent of girls in the fourth grade have attempted to diet because they see themselves as fat.[5] One elementary school girl justified her dieting by saying she just wanted to be skinny so that no one would tease her. How sad it is that children in this culture have been taught to hate their bodies—to measure their worth by comparison to a standard that they can never achieve. At a time when they should be busy being kids, they're worried about how much they weigh, how they look, and how they're seen by others.

For young girls, this insistence on being thin is magnified by the cruelties of childhood. Dozens of studies now show that overweight children are held in low regard by their peers, even at an early age. According to one investigation, silhouettes of obese children were described by six-year-olds as "lazy," "stupid," and "ugly."

This overemphasis on beauty does not occur in a vacuum, of course. Our children have caught our prejudices and our system of values. We, too, measure human worth largely on a scale of physical attractiveness. It's bad enough when adults evaluate each other that way. It's tragic when millions of children have already concluded that they're hopelessly flawed, even before life has gotten started.

View from the Emergency Room

Many of us know the trauma of rushing our young ones off to the local emergency room for trauma care. We usually encounter crowded waiting rooms and frustrating forms to fill out, and all the while we're wondering, "What's wrong with my child?" and "How bad is he or she hurt?"

A typical inner-city emergency room will see about four thousand patients per month. While you and I are sleeping peacefully at two a.m., the emergency room can be a hubbub of activity—with anything from people who have merely cut themselves while washing dishes to victims of serious car accidents or crime. Medical teams attempt as best they can to meet each patient's needs within a few critical minutes.

My friend, emergency-room physician Dr. Elsburg Clark, has been alarmed over the past few years by the growing number of patients, especially children, whose lives are endangered by household drugs, poisonous chemicals, unsupervised swimming pools, and accidental shootings. Many times he has had the unenviable task of telling families that their little one is not going to come home. It's made him much more protective of his own kids, and he strongly suggests basic things that parents can do to help avoid medical emergencies.

It's not new advice, but we need to hear it again. Lock away all medicines, chemicals, and flammable substances. Get rid of slippery rugs and wobbly ladders. Build strong fences around swimming pools, and secure the gate above the reach of young children. And by all means, unload all guns and keep them under lock and key.

Let's make our homes safe havens in which our boys and girls can grow in safety.

Children and Exercise

A medical study conducted at Columbia Children's Hospital in Ohio has confirmed that today's children are heavier and have significantly higher cholesterol and triglyceride levels than kids did even fifteen years ago. One of the researchers, Dr. Hugh Allens, said, "Unless these trends change, 30 million of the 80 million children alive today in the United States will eventually die of heart disease."[6]

Dr. Allens said, "Kids need to turn off the TV, get off the couch." The problem is that high-fat junk food has replaced good nutrition. And even when healthy foods are consumed, kids are not exercising the calories off. Between television, car pools, computer games, and just hanging out at the pizza parlor, kids just don't run and jump like they used to.

So Mom and Dad should find energetic activities to do together with kids. Things like walking and bicycling and playing catch, or hiking. Parents can also get their children involved in community or school sports programs, ranging from softball to soccer.

Children are busy forming habits for a lifetime, so eating right and exercising every day will contribute to greater health in the future. And once your children are on the right path, you might want to begin working on yourself.

A Word for Alcoholics

A company president was asked to fill out a government form that asked, "How many employees do you have—broken down by sex?" He replied, "None that I know of. Our big problem here is alcohol."

Actually, the problem of alcoholism in our society is no laughing matter, especially when you consider the havoc that's wreaked by this addiction. But how does one know when he or she has crossed the line from being a social drinker to being a full-blown alcoholic?

The first red flag is a tolerance for alcohol. The person finds that he has to drink more to achieve the same result. He brags about being able to hold his liquor—as though that were something to be proud of. In reality, showing a tolerance for booze is a dangerous indicator that a chemical adjustment has been made.

Secondly, the alcoholic doesn't want to talk about his drinking. This is the beginning of denial that may be with him for years to come. Next, he begins to experience blackouts. And finally, he is helpless to control how much he drinks once he gets started.

If that profile describes you or a loved one, don't waste another day. Call Alcoholics Anonymous or a center that specializes in treating this disease. You and your family will never regret taking that first step toward recovery.

Needle Park

Perhaps you've noted that some legislators are again toying with the idea of legalizing drugs and offering free needle-exchange programs. The idea is to slow the spread of AIDS and to take the profit out of the drug business. Their argument is seductive, but it is dangerous in my view.

Before such programs are initiated, officials should review the experience of the Swiss. In the late 1980s they set aside city property where addicts could legally shoot up and where free needles were provided, no questions asked. The area of Platzspitz became known as "Needle Park," and it went terribly wrong. Before long, the number of druggies visiting the park soared from two hundred to twenty thousand.[7]

Ten thousand "consumption events" occurred per day, as users from all over Switzerland came to get in on the fun. They soon outnumbered even the local population. The death rate rose as health officials sought to resuscitate as many as forty-five overdose cases per day. And, as should have been expected, the crime rate went through the roof.

City officials finally called off the experiment and closed the park. Almost immediately the crime rate dropped to its former levels, and the program ended in total failure.[8] Even if the plan had worked, it sent this message to kids: "Don't use drugs, but here's what you'll need to do it."

There has to be a better answer than this to one of the greatest curses of our time. I hope our decision makers won't make the same blunder!

Preventing Deafness

I want to offer a word of caution today about excessive noise—especially that which bombards the ears of our kids. Otologists tell us that because our hearing apparatus is a mechanical instrument that is subject to wear, overuse is often related to deafness in old age.

This fact was demonstrated by a study of natives living in a quiet village in an isolated Amazon rain forest. They rarely heard noises louder than a squawking parrot or the sounds of children laughing and playing. Not surprisingly, their hearing remained almost perfect into old age. There was virtually no deafness known to the tribe.

By contrast, living in a noisy environment continually operates the three delicate bones in the middle ear and decreases hearing acuity. Motorcycles, garbage trucks, television, and high-powered machines all take their toll. But children and young people are particularly at risk because of their music. You can imagine the effect of an iPod or MP3 player blasting away at their ears for a decade or more.

Attending a Rolling Stones concert is equivalent to being strapped to the bottom of a jet airplane that is taking off or to being tied to the hood of a Mack truck going sixty miles an hour. Pete Townsend, lead singer of the legendary rock group The Who, is almost totally deaf in one ear from standing near powerful sound equipment.[9]

Quite obviously, parents should try to protect the hearing of their children. That's a tough assignment in today's youth culture, but it's worth the effort.

A Little Bit Helps

Have you noticed that most fitness fanatics are in their early twenties and in the bloom of health? They're not the ones primarily in need of exercise. It's us older folks who need help. Unfortunately, most of us in our forties, fifties, and sixties don't want to move unless absolutely necessary. One woman told me she had made a lifelong commitment not to sweat. Another lady said the only reason for jogging is to look better at her funeral. And a driver put this bumper sticker on his car: I'm pushing 50, and that's exercise enough.

For those who dislike jogging or pumping weights, let me offer some good news. A recent medical study found that it doesn't take much activity to improve general health and vastly reduce the risk of a fatal heart attack. An investigation conducted at the University of Minnesota revealed that work done around the house is sufficient to yield dramatic benefits. The researchers found that men and women who spent an average of forty-seven minutes a day on household chores, such as mowing the lawn, gardening, or just puttering around the house, enjoyed greater longevity than those who were inactive. It's even better if you do some push-ups and sit-ups every few days, but not necessary.[10]

So put down the remote control, get off the couch, and do a little home cleanup or repair. Not only will your house look better, but you're likely to live longer if you do.

Steroid Madness

A new threat to the health of young female athletes has come to light. A study published in the Archives of Pediatric and Adolescent Medicine has revealed that high school girls are using anabolic steroids in greater numbers than previously known.

With the opportunity for college scholarships and even professional sports careers for women, the incentives to build more muscle are irresistible to some teenagers—and perhaps even to their parents. Steroids are also used to help them achieve the "lean" look idealized by the entertainment and fashion industries. Whatever the motivation, three national surveys confirmed that 175,000 American high school females, or 2.4 percent, say they have used steroids at least once. Twice as many boys have experimented with the drugs, but until now it was believed that usage was rare among girls.

Please listen to this, parents: Lifelong physical problems befall those who take steroids. For girls, it can mean a general masculinization of features, including male hair growth, deepening of the voice, shrinkage of the breasts, and menstrual problems. These effects are permanent, like a tattoo that will be with them forever. More serious problems, including liver, cardiovascular, and reproductive illnesses, are also common.[11]

The bottom line is this: Steroid usage is disastrous for females as well as for males.

14

INDEPENDENCE

The Battle for Control

Everybody understands that teenagers are itching to get out on their own—to run their own lives and not have parents telling them what to do anymore. But this yearning for control actually starts much earlier. It's a fundamental dimension of the human personality.

I remember one mother of a tough little four-year-old girl who was demanding her own way. The mother said, "Now, Jenny, you're just going to have to obey me. I'm your boss, and I have the responsibility to lead you, and that's what I intend to do!"

Little Jenny thought over her mother's words for a minute, and then she said, "How long does it have to be that way?"

Already, at four years of age, this child was yearning for a day of freedom when nobody could tell her what to do. Something deep within her spirit was reaching out for control. She shares that yearning with millions of her age-mates—some more than others. The task for us as parents is to hang on to the reins of authority in the early days, even though little hands are trying to pry our fingers loose, and then gradually grant independence as maturity arrives. But this is the most delicate responsibility in parenting. Power granted too early produces folly, but power granted too late brings rebellion.

It is a wise mother or father who can let go little by little as the growing child is able to stand on his or her own. If you watch and listen carefully, the critical milestones will be obvious.

The Wrenching Task of Letting Go

One of the most difficult responsibilities parents face is the task of letting go.

When children are young, Mom and Dad are busy providing love, protection, and authority for them. It seems as though those responsibilities will go on forever. But very quickly, their sons and daughters reach the late teens and early twenties when the door must be fully opened to the world outside. It's the most frightening time of parenthood.

The tendency is to retain control in order to prevent the budding young adults from making mistakes. However, our grown kids are more likely to make the proper choices if they aren't forced to rebel in order to gain their freedom. The simple truth is that responsibility and maturity thrive best in an atmosphere of freedom.

One further word of advice should be offered. A sudden release from all parental guidance and direction at the end of childhood carries dangerous implications. We've all seen individuals who went a little crazy when they were put on their own for the first time. It's much better to grant independence little by little, through the years, as our kids are able to handle a new responsibility. The final release, then, should represent a small step toward freedom rather than a tumble off the cliff into anarchy.

The goal is simple. We need to cut loose the strings of authority little by little so that when our children are beyond the reach of our authority, they no longer need it.

Preparing for College

If your son or daughter is college bound, you've probably spent hours filling out forms, discussing loans, and deciding which colleges to visit. But there are a few more ways you can help prepare for this first experience away from home.

For starters, author Joan Wester Anderson suggests that you make sure that your teen has the basic skills necessary to survive dorm life. Can he or she operate a washer and dryer, stick to a budget, handle a checkbook, get along with roommates, and manage his or her time wisely?

It's important as well to prepare your son or daughter for the negative aspects of campus life. Too often, adults present a rosy portrait of college as "the best years of life," which creates unrealistic expectations that lead to disappointment. Remind your child that homesickness is to be expected and that he or she can call home anytime, just to chat.

It's helpful to talk about those matters beforehand. During the first semester away, letters and treats from home can ease the pain of separation anxiety. And be enthusiastic when that son or daughter returns for visits. If she feels like an intruder, she just might decide to visit someone else's home for future vacations.

Going away to college is a milestone for everyone. With proper planning, it can be an even more positive time of growth for the whole family.

Freedom and Independence

How does a child learn to handle freedom and independence? It ought to occur little by little as the years unfold. The goal is to prepare a child carefully for that moment of release when he or she is beyond the reach of the parent.

I learned this principle from my own mother, who made a calculated effort to teach independence and responsibility. After laying a foundation during the younger years, she gave me a "final examination" when I was seventeen years old. Mom and Dad went on a two-week trip and left me at home with the family car and permission to have my buddies stay at the house. Wow! Fourteen slumber parties in a row! I couldn't believe it. We could have gone crazy and torn the place apart, but we didn't. We behaved rather responsibly.

I always wondered why my mother took such a risk, and after I was grown, I asked her about it. She just smiled and said, "I knew in one year you would be leaving for college, where you would have complete freedom with no one watching over you. I wanted to expose you to that independence while you were still under my influence."

You see, my mother employed an important child-rearing principle in that instance. For years she had been consciously preparing me for the coming independence.

If you have children, let them test the waters of freedom as they're growing up, rather than thrusting them into the big wide ocean all at once. Then when they're on their own and completely emancipated, they'll know how to handle the experience responsibly and wisely.

Rumspringa

The task of letting go of our grown children after adolescence is one of the most difficult assignments in the entire realm of parenting. The duel dangers, of course, are doing it either too early or too late. Let me tell you how the Amish turn loose their children.

They keep their children under very tight control when they are young. Strict discipline and harsh standards of behavior are imposed from infancy. But when children turn sixteen years of age, they enter a period called "Rumspringa." Suddenly, all restrictions are lifted. They are free to drink, smoke, or behave in ways that horrify their parents. Some do just that. Most don't. They're even granted the right to leave the Amish community if they choose. But if they stay, it must be in accordance with the social order. The majority accept the heritage of their families, not because they must, but because they choose to.

Although I admire the Amish and many of their approaches to child rearing, I believe the Rumspringa concept is implemented too precipitously for children raised in a more open society. I've seen families grant "instant adulthood" to their adolescents, to their families' regret.

Instead, I recommend that parents begin transferring tiny elements of independence literally in toddlerhood. Each year more responsibility and freedom must be given to the child so that the final release in early adulthood is merely a small step rather than a leap off a cliff.

Give 'Em a Push!

Some teenagers can't wait to get out of the house and on their own. Others don't go quite as willingly. How do you get your grown child to move on when the time has come?

Sometimes independence eludes young adults not because parents withhold it but because sons and daughters refuse to accept it. They have no intention of growing up, and why should they? The nest is just too comfortable at home. Food is prepared. Clothes are laundered, and bills are paid. There's no incentive to face the cold world of reality, and they are determined not to budge. Some even refuse to work. I know it's difficult to dislodge a homebound son or daughter. They're like furry little puppies who hang around the back door waiting for a saucer of warm milk. But to let them stay year after year, especially if they're not pursuing career goals, is to cultivate irresponsibility and dependency. That's not love, even though it may feel like it. There comes the time when you must gently but forthrightly hand the reins over to your child and force him to stand on his own. You might even have to help him pack.

JOY

Sunday, a Day of Rest

Remember when the world seemed to slow down on Sundays? Monday through Friday were for work and school. Saturday was for chores. And Sunday…well, Sunday was a quieter day when things geared down for the world to catch its breath. But with the passage of time, Sunday began to lose its significance. Now we huff and puff seven days a week, hurtling down the road toward burnout or even an early demise. I'd like to make a case once more for setting aside one day per week for rest, relaxation, and worship.

I've recently been privileged to spend some time with Truett Cathy, the founder and CEO of the Chick-fil-A restaurant corporation. When he began his business in the 1950s, he determined that he would close all of his stores on Sunday, regardless of the circumstances. Then it was an accepted practice. Now it's extremely unusual, especially for a restaurant chain with many outlets in malls. To this day, Cathy has never wavered from his commitment. He told me he believes Sunday is a special day, a day set apart from the rest of the week.

Sound old-fashioned? Well, perhaps. But maybe it's one traditional idea that still has a place today. Why don't you try gearing down just a bit this next Sunday? The fourth commandment instructs us to do just that.

Holiday Brattiness

Erma Bombeck once wrote, "The family that plays together, fights together," and I'm afraid she was right.[1]

Why is it that children are often the most obnoxious and irritating on vacations and at other times when parents specifically try to please them? On those special days, you'd think the kids would say to themselves, "Wow! Mom and Dad are doing something really nice for us, taking us on this great vacation. We're going to give them a break and be really good kids today."

Unfortunately, children just don't think that way. Why is this? One reason, I think, is because children often feel compelled to reexamine the boundaries whenever they think they may have moved. In other words, whenever the normal routine changes, kids often push the limits to see just what they can get away with.

So how can parents preserve their own peace of mind and maintain harmony during car trips and family holidays? Well, sometimes it helps to redefine the boundaries at the beginning of your time together. Let the kids know exactly what you're doing and what's expected of them. If they still misbehave, respond with good, loving discipline right from the start.

No parent wants to be an ogre on vacation, but it helps to show a little firmness at the outset that can make the rest of the time together fun for the entire family.

Toddlerhood Traumas

Wouldn't it be interesting to hold a national convention sometime, bringing together all the mothers who have experienced the particular traumas of raising one or more toddlers?

If that occurred, we'd hear some amazingly similar stories. Hasn't every mother opened a bedroom door unexpectedly to find her little tiger covered with lipstick from the top of her pink head to the soles of her sneakers? On the wall is her own artistic creation with a red handprint right in the center, and throughout the room is the aroma of perfume with which she has just anointed her baby brother.

What should you do if you find yourself in this situation? Sure, there's a mess to be cleaned up, but I hope you would find humor in the experience. And why not? Laughter can be the key to survival during the stresses of raising kids. If you can see the delightful side of your assignment, you can also deal with the difficult side. Almost every day I hear from mothers who have learned to use the ballast of humor to keep their boats afloat. They know that these child-rearing years will be but a dim memory in a brief moment or two.

As the father of two grown children, let me urge the parents of young children to hug 'em while you can. They'll be grown before you know it.

Return to Mayberry

When it comes to family-related matters, I'm known as a traditionalist. In fact, there are some who think I would like to take the American family back to the days of Ozzie and Harriet. But that criticism is preposterous.

I don't want to go back to Ozzie and Harriet. I want to go back to Mayberry—with Sheriff Andy Taylor and the gang. I loved it when Barney Fife said, "My whole body's a weapon!"

Obviously, I know that Mayberry never existed—that Aunt Bea and Opie were figments of the writers' imagination. But there is validity to the theme of that sitcom. I was in high school during the "happy days" of the 1950s, and I can tell you that it was much easier to grow up in that era. I attended a racially mixed high school, yet there were no gangs there, very little alcohol, and absolutely *no* drugs. None! Most of us studied hard enough to get by, and we rather liked our parents. As for sex, there was far more talk about it than action. About once a year a girl came up pregnant; but she was packed off somewhere, and I never knew where she went. By almost any measure, kids simply fared better in those days.

Nevertheless, that era is gone forever. You can't back up on a freeway. But considering the enormous pressures on today's generation, we could make the world safer and more secure for them. And the way to start is by building stronger and more harmonious families in which they can grow.

Exploring the World of Nature

Teaching children to appreciate nature is one of the most enjoyable tasks of parenting. It's also one of the simplest, since children are naturally curious about the world around them.

When I was very young, I had a fascination with red ants. We had a big two-gallon fruit jar that I used for an ant farm. I'd fill it with dirt, then collect thousands of red ants and put them inside. I'd keep them for months at a time, watching them dig chambers and compartments and trails. Apart from being stung a few hundred times, it was a successful project. And it helped instill in me a sense of wonder at nature and creation that has continued to this day.

When you start teaching your own child about nature, I suggest you capitalize on her own curiosity. If she walks into the house with an earthworm or a frog in her hand, see it as an opportunity. Our own two-year-old once asked his mother if worms could yawn. She was unprepared for the inquiry.

If you have a backyard, walk around with your child and look under the leaves and rocks just to see what you can find. Even in a small window box, you can grow a garden and teach the miracle of plant life from seed to harvest. It only takes a little effort to kindle in your child a lasting fascination with the beauty of the natural world.

A Poem

Someone sent me this anonymous little poem the other day that I want to share with you. I don't know who wrote the piece, but I think you're going to like it.

> If you can start the day without caffeine; if you can get going without pep pills; if you can always be cheerful, ignoring aches and pains; if you can resist complaining and boring people with your troubles; if you can eat the same food every day and be grateful for it; if you can understand when your loved ones are too busy to give you any time; if you can forgive a friend's lack of consideration; if you can overlook it when those you love take it out on you when, through no fault of your own, something goes wrong; if you can take criticism and blame without resentment; if you can ignore a friend's limited education and never correct him; if you can resist treating a rich friend better than a poor friend; if you can face the world without lies and deceit; if you can conquer tension without medical help; if you can relax without liquor; if you can sleep without the aid of drugs; if you can honestly say that deep in your heart you have no prejudice against creed or color, religion or politics; then, my friend, you're almost as good as your dog. Almost, but not quite.[2]

This poem is dedicated to every dog lover in the world.

Kids Say the Neatest Things

I love kids, don't you? I like the way they think, the way they talk, and I especially like to read the things that they and their parents write and say.

For example, an eight-year-old girl named Brandy wrote to thank us for a magazine we publish called *Clubhouse.* She said, "Thanks for letting me join in the *clud,* and thanks to my aunt. You guys are really nicie. I enjoy those mageniens. My hoby is cletting rocks, and stunding about the rain fostes. And my favorite subject in school is spelling."

Another little girl came home from the pediatrician and told her daddy that she got shots that day for "mumps, measles, and rebellion." Don't you wish we had an inoculation for that?

And then a mother wrote to say this: "Perhaps there should be a uniform word for 'potty' when children have to go to the bathroom. My three-year-old has been taught to refer to that act as 'a whisper.' Well, his grandfather came to visit us, and in the middle of the night my son came to his bed and said, 'Grandpa, I have to whisper.' Well, not wanting to awaken his wife he said, 'OK. Whisper in my ear.' And he did."

These delightful moments are what make child rearing so much fun. If your kids have said funny or clever things, I wish you'd send some of those quotes to me.

LEGACY

Preserving Your Family Heritage

The lyrics of an African folk song say that when an old person dies, it's as if a library has burned down. It is true. There's a richness of family heritage in each person's life that will be lost if it isn't passed on to the next generation.

To preserve this heritage for our children we must tell them where we've been and how we got to this moment. Sharing about our faith, about our early family experiences, about the obstacles we overcame or the failures we suffered, can bring a family together and give it a sense of identity.

My great-grandmother (Nanny), who helped raise me when I was a boy, was nearly one hundred years old when she died. I loved for her to tell me tales about her early life on the frontier. A favorite story focused on the mountain lions that would prowl around her log cabin at night and attack the livestock. She could hear them growling and moving past her window as she lay in bed. Nanny's father would try to chase the cats away with his rifle before they killed a pig or a goat. I would sit fascinated as this sweet lady described a world that had long vanished by the time I came on the scene. Her accounts of plains life helped open me to a love of history, a subject that still fascinates me to this day.

The stories of your past, of your childhood, of the courtship with your spouse, and so on can be treasures to your children. Unless you share those experiences with them, that part of their history will be gone forever. Take the time to make yesterday come alive for the kids in your family.

The Magnificent Flying Machine

I s your family soaring above the clouds right now—or are you weighed down by activities, appointments, and acquisitions?

My friend Dennis Rainey tells the story of *Double Eagle Two,* the first hot-air balloon to cross the Atlantic Ocean. The men piloting the magnificent craft caught an air corridor that carried them all the way across the Atlantic. But when they were just off the coast of Ireland, they flew into heavy cloud cover, and ice began to form on the balloon's outer shell. They lost altitude, dropping from twenty thousand to ten thousand feet in a matter of hours.

The crew did everything they could to save the balloon. They threw over video cameras, food rations, and even a glider with which they had planned to land. At about four thousand feet, they transmitted their location, and then they threw the radio overboard. Finally, at three thousand feet, they broke through into sunlight. The ice came off in sheets, and the great balloon soared all the way into France.

Something similar to this scenario is repeated in homes today. The "family balloon" is encumbered by responsibilities, pressures, obligations, schedules, and entanglements. More and more activities are taken on board, causing the balloon to wobble and lose altitude. Many crash in the sea before they recognize the need to lighten the load.

There's a time to cut back, to simplify, to say no, and to spend more time at home. Then we can soar above the clouds, free and unencumbered by the things that would weigh us down.

A Child's View of Grandma

Many years ago, a four-year-old girl named Sandra Louise Doty sat on a stool in a florist's shop while her grandmother made arrangements for customers. As the grandmother and granddaughter chatted, the child began describing what she thought a grandmother was like. The older woman wrote down Sandra's words, which have been quoted around the world. Sandra is now Mrs. Andrew De Mattia, and has given us permission to share with you her original composition entitled, "What a Grandmother Is."

The little girl said, "A grandmother is a lady who has no children of her own, so she likes other people's little girls. A grandfather is a man grandmother. He goes for walks with the boys, and they talk about fishing and tractors and things like that. Grandmas don't have to do anything except be there. They're old, so they shouldn't play hard or run. It is enough if they drive us to the market where the pretend horse is and have lots of dimes ready. Or if they take us for walks, they should slow down past things like pretty leaves or caterpillars. They should never, ever say hurry up.

"Usually, they are fat, but not too fat to tie kids' shoes. They wear glasses and funny underwear. They can take off their teeth and gums. They don't have to be smart, only answer questions like why dogs hate cats and how come God isn't married? They don't talk baby talk like visitors do, because it is hard to understand. When they read to us they don't skip or mind if it is the same story again."

Then she finished, "Everybody should try to have [a grandmother], especially if you don't have television, because grandmas are the only grown-ups who have got time."

Sandra has told us what children value most in adults: one who is kind, appreciates the finer things of life, and isn't too busy to love a kid.

The Wonders of God's Creation

Recently I heard an incredible story of the perseverance of Pacific salmon from a nature video produced by the Moody Institute of Science. A salmon was spawned in a hatchery in northern California, released into a channel which led to a stream, the stream to a river, and the river to the Pacific Ocean. After becoming ocean-bound, the fish swam thousands of miles. Then, as if by command, she began a treacherous journey back to the place of her spawning. The fish relocated not only the spot where she'd entered the ocean but the river, the stream, and the exact inlet from which she had been released.

Now, here's the almost unbelievable part of the story. The salmon worked her way up through a drain and pushed through a heavy screened lid on top of a three-foot vertical pipe, all to end up in the very same tank from which she was hatched. Special markings on her fin confirmed the amazing journey.

As I thought about this feat, it occurred to me that there is, perhaps, a parallel between the early life of the salmon and the impact we, as parents, have on our children. Our kids are shaped forever by the love and training received at home. They will always be influenced by the experiences that characterized the family in which they were raised. Not one experience is ever completely lost. Even at fifty years of age, they will "remember" and be guided by that which was taught in childhood. It's an awesome thought.

My Friend Wendy

The year was 1983, and I had an appointment with a young woman who had asked to see me. I was about to meet one of the most unforgettable people I would ever be privileged to know.

Wendy Bergren, the mother of three beautiful little girls, was dying of breast cancer. Doctors had confirmed that the disease was terminal and advised her to go home and prepare to die. But Wendy wouldn't accept their advice. She sought out physicians who would treat her aggressively with chemotherapy, radiation, or anything that might buy a little time. She accepted the certainty of death, but this young mother was determined to live long enough for her newborn baby to remember her. Despite the ordeal that followed, Wendy would not yield to depression and despair. She concentrated, not on herself, but on her children and others in difficult situations. She published a little booklet that listed twenty ways to reach out to families that were struggling from debilitating illnesses. To the end, Wendy was still trying to help those who were hurting.

My young friend died on February 12, 1985. She was courageous to the end. Wendy left behind a loving husband, Scott, and three beautiful, healthy girls. They're grown now, and I'm dedicating this commentary to Chrissy, Casey, and Dianna.

How to Help a Sick Mom

In the previous commentary, I wrote about a remarkable young woman named Wendy Bergren, who suffered from terminal breast cancer. In the midst of her terrible ordeal, she penned a little booklet based on her own experience. Her purpose was to offer advice to friends and relatives of mothers with cancer. Wendy listed twenty suggestions to help sick moms and undergird their families when debilitating disease lingers on.

For example, Wendy suggested that friends make it possible for the children of sick mothers to attend birthday parties by bringing some gifts that have already been wrapped for use when needed. And she thought it would be a good idea to make cookie dough and bring it frozen, so sick moms could have the pleasure of baking something fresh for their children.

Wendy also suggested that friends talk about the future. Wendy wrote: "Talk about next week. Next year, ten or twenty years! The power of planning is incredible. Talk to me about my baby's senior graduation, and I can get through next week. Bring travel folders for my silver anniversary trip, or discuss hairstyles for when my hair grows back in. If you look ahead, I can too."

There were seventeen additional suggestions in Wendy's little booklet, but the reader can understand her message. Her purpose was to share her experience with others. This courageous woman brought comfort and kindness to many in the closing days of her life.

Wendy Bergren is gone now, but she will never be forgotten.[1]

A Model Soldier

One of my heroes was the great military leader General Douglas MacArthur. He led the Allies to victory over the Japanese during World War II and later commanded the United Nations forces in Korea. MacArthur's surprise landing of his troops at Inchon was one of the most brilliant maneuvers in history. Undoubtedly, he was one of our greatest and most revered military leaders.

I also admire the memory of MacArthur for his respect for families. He was honored in 1942, for example, for being a good father.[2] He was asked to speak on that occasion and made this statement:

> Nothing has touched me more deeply than the act of the National Father's Day committee. By profession, I am a soldier and take great pride in that fact. But I am prouder, infinitely prouder, to be a father. A soldier destroys in order to build. The father only builds, never destroys. The one has the potentialities of death, the other embodies creation and life. And while the hordes of death are mighty, the battalions of life are mightier still. It is my hope that my son, when I am gone, will remember me not from the battle, but in the home.[3]

Like the old general, I will consider that my earthly existence will have been wasted unless I succeed as a husband and father, and only if God is ultimately pleased with me. There is no higher calling to which I could aspire.

The Battle of the Somme

Though the world has largely forgotten it, July 1 is the anniversary of one of the worst military catastrophes in human history. It is called the Battle of the Somme, and it took place in France during the First World War.

On that day the Allied commander, General Douglas Haig, foolishly ordered more than 100,000 men to charge across "no man's land" just after dawn. The German army knew that an attack was coming, and they crisscrossed the battlefield with machine-gun fire, systematically mowing down the heavily laden troops. It was the bloodiest day in British history, with nearly twenty thousand men killed and thirty-five thousand wounded. The French and German troops suffered comparable casualties.[4]

The tragedy of the Somme was its utter waste of human lives. The battle continued for one hundred forty days and soon involved some three million men. More than a third of them became casualties before it was over. And for what? The Allies never drove the Germans back more than seven miles at any point, and even that ground was lost in 1918.[5]

Oh, I know this all happened long ago and far away. What does it matter today? But somehow it seems fitting for us to pause for a moment to remember the sacrifice of the men who died and the four million family members whose beloved husbands, sons, and fathers never returned. It all began at dawn on July 1, 1916.

Christmas Memories

Without a doubt, the best time of the year for shared memories is Christmas. Some of my happiest memories, both as a child and as an adult, have been rooted in the Christmas season. I remember the year my father went to the bank and bought twenty new, crisp one-dollar bills back in the days when a dollar would buy a meal. He attached a Merry Christmas note to each dollar and handed them out; one apiece to the newsboy, the shoeshine man, the postman, and seventeen others. He was merely thanking them for being his friends.

Another memory occurred many years later. My wife, our two children, and I had boarded a plane for Kansas City to spend the holidays with my parents. When I stepped off the plane and into the terminal, I instantly caught sight of my six-foot-four-inch father towering over the crowd. There was a twinkle in his eyes and a smile on his face, and Mom, of course, was aglow with excitement. Her family had come home for Christmas. That scene is videotaped in my mind today. Now those good people are gone, and only the memory lingers on.

During the Christmas season, I hope your own times of excitement and sharing and fellowship will leave you with a special gift…memories that will last a lifetime.

LIFE LESSONS

Grabbing Those Teachable Moments

Years ago, my teenage son and I got up one morning and situated ourselves in a deer blind before the break of day. About twenty yards away from us was a feeder that operated on a timer. At seven a.m., it automatically dropped kernels of corn into a pan below. Ryan and I huddled together in the blind, talking softly about whatever came to mind. Then through the fog, we saw a beautiful doe emerge. She came silently into the clearing and moved toward the feeder. We had no intention of shooting her, of course, but it was fun to watch this beautiful animal from close range. The doe ate a quick breakfast and fled.

I whispered to Ryan, "There's something valuable to be learned from what we've just seen. Whenever you find a free supply of high-quality corn unexpectedly provided right there in the middle of the forest, be careful. The people who put it there are probably sitting nearby just waiting to take a shot at you."

Ryan may not always remember that advice, but I will. It isn't often that a father says something that he considers to be profound to his teenage son. One thing is certain: This interchange and the other ideas that we shared on that day would not have occurred at home. Opportunities for that kind of communication have to be created. Those teachable moments occur when you have set aside time to be with people you love, especially your children. Preserve them at all cost.

Whomever

My family and I took a ski vacation in California some years ago when our children were still young. It was a memorable time but one that had its frustrating moments. Coping with two kids who are complaining about the cold and losing gloves and scarves can get on a father's nerves.

After getting them located at the lodge, I parked the car and waited for a flatbed truck to take me back to the top of the mountain. About fifteen young skiers waited with me. Then I noticed a girl in her early twenties standing with the others. When she turned to look at me, I recognized the unmistakable appearance of mental retardation in her eyes. She was behaving strangely and repeating the word *whomever* without meaning. The other young skiers smiled and rolled their eyes.

Then I noticed that the big man standing near her was her father. He had obviously seen the reactions of the other skiers. Then he did something that moved me. He put his arms around the girl, looked down lovingly at his daughter, and said, "Yeah, babe. Whomever."

This father had obviously seen the scorn in the faces of the other skiers. The compassion in his voice and his manner seemed to be saying, "Yes, it's true. She is retarded. We can't hide that fact. She is very limited in ability. She won't sing the songs. She won't write the books. In fact, she's already out of school. We've done the best we could for her. But I want you all to know something. This is my girl, and I love her. She's the whole world to me. And I'm not ashamed to be identified with her. 'Yeah, babe. Whomever!'"[1]

The tenderness of that father flooded out from his soul and engulfed mine. I quietly apologized to the Lord for complaining about my irritations and looked forward to hugging my children at the top of the mountain.

Jeep Fenders

Children can be hateful to each other, especially when adults haven't taught them basic kindness and sensitivity. I learned that when I was only eight years old.

I regularly attended a Sunday school in those days, and a visitor entered the class one morning and sat down. He said his name was Fred. I can still see his face. More important, I can still see Fred's ears. They were curved in the shape of a C and protruded noticeably. For some reason they reminded me of Jeep fenders. Without thinking of Fred's feelings, I pointed out this strange characteristic to my friends, who all thought "Jeep Fenders" was a terribly funny name for a boy with bent ears. Fred seemed to think it was funny, too, and he chuckled along with the rest of us.

Suddenly, Fred stopped laughing. He jumped to his feet, red in the face (and ears), and rushed to the door, crying. He bolted into the hall and ran from the building. Fred never returned to our class. I remember my shock over Fred's violent and unexpected reaction. I had no idea that I was embarrassing him by my little joke. Looking back on the episode, however, I believe that my teachers and parents were largely responsible for that event. They should have told me what it feels like to be laughed at, especially when it concerns something different about our bodies.

Children can be taught to be sensitive to the feelings of others. But in the absence of that teaching, they can be brutal to one another. Another "Jeep Fenders" is out there somewhere today. Protect him or her from ridicule!

Quantity Versus Quality at Home

It's not the quantity of time that you spend with your children, it's the quality that counts. Or is it?

Maybe you've heard the argument that it doesn't matter how little time you spend with your children as long as your few moments together are especially meaningful. But the logic of that concept seems suspect to me. The question is, Why do we have to choose between the virtues of quantity versus quality? We won't accept that forced choice in any other area of our lives. So why is it only relevant to our children?

Let me illustrate my point. Let's suppose you've looked forward all day to eating at one of the finest restaurants in town. The waiter brings you a menu, and you order the most expensive steak in the house. But when the meal arrives, you see a tiny piece of meat about one inch square in the center of the plate. When you complain about the size of the steak, the waiter says, "Sir, I recognize that the portion is small, but that's the finest corn-fed beef money can buy. You'll never find a better bite of meat than we've served you tonight. As to the portion, I hope you understand that it's not the quantity that matters, it's the quality that counts."

You would object, and for good reason. Why? Because both quality and quantity are important in many areas of our lives, including how we relate to children. They need our time and the best we have to give them.

My concern is that the "quantity versus quality" argument might be a poorly disguised rationalization for giving our children—neither.

The Bulldog and the Scottie

When I was about ten years old, I loved a couple of dogs that belonged to two families in our neighborhood. One was a black Scottie who liked to retrieve tennis balls, and the other was a pug bulldog who had a notoriously bad temper.

One day as I was tossing the ball for the Scottie, I decided to throw it in the direction of the grouch. It was an awful mistake. The bulldog grabbed the Scottie by the throat and wouldn't let go. Neighbors came running as the Scottie screamed in pain. It took ten minutes and a garden hose to pry loose the bulldog's grip, and by then the Scottie was almost dead. He spent two weeks in the vet hospital, and I spent two weeks in the "doghouse." I regret throwing that ball to this day.

I've thought about that experience many times and its application to human relationships. Indeed, it is a simple thing to precipitate a fight. All that's necessary is to toss a ball, symbolically, under the more aggressive of the two. This is done by revealing negative comments made by one or by baiting the first in the presence of the other. It can also be accomplished very easily in business by assigning overlapping territory to two managers.

Again, the leader can start a terrible fight by tossing a ball in the right (or wrong) direction. The natural jealousy and antagonism of competitors will do the rest.

The Little Girl in the Airport

You can learn a great deal by watching people, which happens to be one of my favorite pastimes. I was doing just that some years ago while waiting to catch a plane at Los Angeles International Airport. Standing near me was an old man, obviously waiting for a passenger who should have been on the plane that had just arrived. At his side was a little girl, who must have been about seven years old. She, too, was looking for a certain face in the crowd. She clung to the old man's arm, whom I assumed to have been her grandfather. They both seemed unusually stressed.

As the last passengers filed by, the girl began to cry. She wasn't merely disappointed in that moment; her little heart was broken. The grandfather also appeared to be fighting back tears. For some reason, he failed to comfort the child, who buried her face in the sleeve of his coat. I wondered what special agony they were going through. Was it the child's mother who failed to show up? Or had the little girl's daddy promised to come and then changed his mind?

The old man and the child waited for yet another plane and then gave up hope. The only sound was the sniffing of the little girl as they walked through the terminal and toward the door. When I last saw her, she was still clutching her grandfather's sleeve.

Where is that child now, who must be in her late twenties? God only knows. Somewhere out there is a young woman with a very bitter memory—one which I happened to have been there to witness.

The Captain and the Seaman

In the official magazine of the Naval Institute, Frank Koch reported on a very unusual encounter at sea. A battleship was coming in for maneuvers in heavy weather. Shortly after the sun went down, the look-out reported a light in the distance, so the captain had the signalman send a message: "We're on a collision course. Advise you to change your course twenty degrees."

Minutes later a signal came back: "Advisable for you to change your course."

The captain angrily ordered that another signal be sent: "I am a captain. Change course twenty degrees."

Again came the reply: "I'm a seaman, second class. You'd better change your course."

Furious by this point, the captain barked a final threat. "I'm a battleship! Change your course!"

The signal came back. "I'm a lighthouse."

The captain changed his course![2]

I don't care how big and powerful a person may become, it's foolhardy to ignore the beacons that warn us of danger. They take various forms: symptoms of health problems, prolonged marital conflict, rebellious children, excessive debt, stress that ties us in knots. These are the warning signs of approaching danger. It matters not that we're successful, influential, and busy. A seaman, second class, sits in a lighthouse somewhere and signals, "Change your course," and the wise captain does so with haste.

Tetherball Terror

I want to say a few words today on behalf of all those noble people who teach our boys and girls in public and private schools. I was also a teacher many years ago, and it was one of the most rewarding things I have ever done—and one of the most challenging.

I remember the morning a kid named Norbert suddenly became ill. He lost his breakfast with no warning to his fellow students or to me. I can still recall thirty-two sixth graders racing to the far corners of the room and shouting, "Eeeeuuuuyuckk!" One of them said, "I wouldn't talk, Greg. You did it last year!"

Then there was the afternoon a twelve-year-old girl named Donna asked if I wanted to play a game of tetherball. "Sure," I said. It was a big mistake. Donna was a tetherball freak. Right there in front of every kid on the playground, she drew back and spiked the ball with all her might and drove it straight up my nose. I never even saw it coming. She had my nose vibrating like a tuning fork.

It was hard on the pride of a twenty-four-year-old would-be jock, I can tell you. But those weren't the toughest aspects about teaching. I learned that it takes tons of patience, love, skill, and dedication to do the job right.

So let me tip my hat today to those men and women who head out each morning for the classroom. The future is in their hands.

One-Horse Open Sleigh

John Pierpont lived and died a failure. At least that's how he might be seen by history. It's not as if he didn't try to find his niche. John poured his heart into everything he did. He just didn't seem to be good at anything.

His career started out with a teaching degree from Yale, but his first position didn't last very long. John was much too easy on his students. So he decided to become a lawyer. He failed at that as well. He opened a dry-goods store but soon went bankrupt. Next, John tried his hand at poetry. He wasn't a bad writer, but he just couldn't earn enough to pay his bills.

John went to school again—this time to become a preacher. His first congregation asked him to resign, so he gave up the ministry. Politics had always intrigued him, so he ran for governor of Massachusetts. He lost big. So he ran for Congress. Again, he lost. Even bigger. Then the Civil War broke out, and he enlisted as a chaplain—but for only two weeks. Eventually, he died at the age of seventy-one while serving as a clerk in the Treasury Department.

John Pierpont's tombstone reads simply: "Poet, preacher, philosopher, philanthropist." Well, one out of four isn't bad. He wrote a simple song somewhere along the way that any three-year-old could sing. The melody and lyrics are as cheerful as Christmas itself. He called it "Jingle Bells," a song about sleighs and horses and snow and laughter.[3]

John Pierpont, though dead and gone, had finally found his niche.

LOVE

Unconditional Love from a Child

We sometimes learn the most from our children.

Some time ago, a friend of mine punished his three-year-old daughter for wasting a roll of gold wrapping paper. Money was tight, and he became infuriated when the child tried to decorate a box to put under the Christmas tree. Nevertheless, the little girl brought the gift to her father the next morning and said, "This is for you, Daddy." He was embarrassed by his earlier overreaction, but his anger flared again when he found that the box was empty.

He yelled at her, "Don't you know that when you give someone a present, there's supposed to be something inside of it?"

The little girl looked up at him with tears in her eyes and said, "Oh, Daddy, it's not empty. I blew kisses in the box. I filled it with my love. All for you, Daddy."

The father was crushed. He put his arms around his little girl, and he begged her for forgiveness. My friend told me that he kept that gold box by his bed for years. Whenever he was discouraged, he would take out an imaginary kiss and remember the love of the child who had put it there.

In a very real sense, each of us as parents has been given a gold container filled with unconditional love and kisses from our children. There is no more precious possession anyone could hold.

A Scrawny Cat

I remember sitting in my car at a fast-food restaurant eating a hamburger and French fries, when I happened to look in the rearview mirror. There I saw the most pitiful, scrawny, dirty little kitten on a ledge behind my car. I was so touched by how hungry he looked that I tore off a piece of my hamburger and tossed it to him. But before this kitten could reach it, a huge gray tomcat sprang out of the bushes, grabbed the morsel, and gobbled it down. I felt so sorry for the little guy, who turned and ran back into the shadows, still hungry and frightened.

I was immediately reminded of my years as a junior high school teacher. I saw teenagers every day who were just as needy, just as deprived, just as lost as that little kitten. It wasn't food that they required; it was love and attention and respect that they needed, and they were desperate for it. And just when they opened up and revealed the pain inside, one of the more popular kids would abuse and ridicule them, sending them scurrying back into the shadows, frightened and alone.

We, as adults, must never forget the pain of trying to grow up and the competitive world in which many adolescents live today. Taking a moment to listen, to care, and to direct such a youngster may be the best investment of a lifetime.

Loving Hands

Human hands. They perform marvelous functions, from those of a concert pianist to those of a brain surgeon. With the thumb in opposition to the fingers to facilitate grasping, and with the concentration of sensory nerves in the pads for evaluating the texture and the temperature of our world, human hands are a marvel of design. But they are much more than precision machinery. They carry great meaning because of what they represent to us eventually.

My mother had soft, feminine hands, and she used them when I was small to stroke my hair and rub my back. Her touch conveyed love to me in a way that compared with nothing else. I remember visiting her in a nursing home shortly before her death and looking again at those familiar hands. They were wrinkled and palsied by that time, yet they were still beautiful to me. How hard she worked to make life easy for me.

What I remember most about my father was the size of his hands. They engulfed mine and made me proud and secure as I trotted along beside him on the street. He used those hands to teach me how to cast with a rod and reel, how to draw and paint. I had seen him hold a King James Bible at least ten thousand times, thoughtfully turning the pages as he studied the Scripture. Soon those beloved hands would be folded across his chest in stillness.

The pressing question for parents is how your children will remember your hands. Hopefully, they will convey warmth, security, and protection. They should provide comfort and affirmation—but never abuse or neglect. If you do your job properly, then your hands, like those of my parents, will leave a lasting legacy of love.

Freedom and Respect

Someone once said, "If you love something, set it free. If it comes back to you, it's yours for life. But if it doesn't come back, it never was yours in the first place." That adage has significant meaning for those who are developing romantic relationships. Let me illustrate.

Some individuals are so needy that they begin to violate the well-known principles of freedom and respect in human interactions. They beg, cry, and grovel for acceptance. Anyone who begins to react that way destroys what is left of the relationship. Just as a drowning person grabs anything that floats, including a rescuer, a panic-stricken lover often tries to hold the one who is attempting to escape. That other person becomes frantic to get away!

I heard about a young man who was determined to win the affection of a girl who refused to even see him. He decided that the way to her heart was through the mail, so he began writing a love letter every day. When she didn't respond, he increased his output to three notes every twenty-four hours. In all, he wrote more than seven hundred letters in a single summer. Not only did his plan not work—she married the postman! That's the way romantic love works. Appearing too anxious and available actually drives people away rather than attracting them into a committed relationship.

In short, romantic love is one of those rare human endeavors that succeed best when they require the least effort. Respect precedes love, and that's why would-be lovers like to nibble at the bait before swallowing the hook.

Mindy

Mindy was neither a purebred nor a champion, as dogs go. Her daddy had been a travelin' man, so we really didn't know much about her heritage. She was just a scared pup who showed up at the front door late one night after being abused by her owners and then thrown out of a car. We didn't really want another dog, but what could we do?

So we took her in, and she quickly grew to become one of the finest dogs we had ever owned. But Mindy never lost that emotional fragility inflicted by abuse. She couldn't stand to be criticized or scolded when she had accidentally done something wrong. She would actually jump into my lap and hide her eyes.

One summer we went away for a two-week vacation and left Mindy in the backyard. A neighbor boy gave her food and water, but otherwise she was alone most of that time. We obviously underestimated her loneliness or what the isolation would do to her. When we returned, we found her lying next to the house on a blanket surrounded by about seven of our daughter's old stuffed animals. Mindy had found them in a box in the garage and carried them one by one to her bed. She had been desperate for friends!

You know, if an old dog needs love and acceptance in this way, how much more true is it of every child who walks the earth? It's our job as adults to see that each one of them receives the security and love that he or she requires.

MARRIAGE

Preparing for the Big Day

Premarital counseling can make a great contribution to the stability of a future relationship. My friend Dr. Archibald Hart, psychologist and author, recommends at least six to eight counseling sessions before the bride and groom meet at the altar. They are needed because those who are engaged often have many expectations about marriage that are never verbalized until after the knot has been tied. Conflict then becomes inevitable when those differing assumptions collide. Therefore, it is important to talk through these understandings in the less antagonistic light of the courtship.

Dr. Hart often asks these kinds of questions to the couples who consult with him:[1]

- "If I had never met the person you're planning to marry, and I had to rely on you to give me a description of who that individual is, what would you tell me?"

- "If you could think of one thing that you would like to see your fiancé change, what would it be?"

- "What are the five or six major goals that have been established for your first few years together?"

- "What does your budget look like?"

- "Have you planned how you're going to pay for the things you're going to buy beyond the honeymoon?"

Tough questions? You bet. But the couple that can't agree on these kinds of issues before they're married is certain to fight over them after the wedding. That's why I often recommend to the parents of engaged couples that they pay for premarital counseling as a wedding gift. It might be the most thoughtful gift you could provide.

Keeping the Boats Together

I magine, if you will, two little rowboats setting off to cross a choppy lake. A man sits in one, and a woman rides blissfully in the other. They have every intention of rowing side by side, but then they begin drifting in opposite directions. They can hardly hear each other above the sound of the wind. Soon the man finds himself at the northern end of the lake, and the woman bobs along at the south. Neither can recall how he or she drifted so far from the other or what they should do to reconnect.

This simple illustration has meaning for newlyweds who embark on life's journey. They stand at the altar and pledge to live together in love and harmony. Unfortunately, it doesn't always work that way. Unless their relationship is maintained and cultivated, it will grow distant and estranged. In essence, that is why romantic little rowboats often drift toward opposite ends of the lake.

The question to be raised is, how can husbands and wives remain in the same proximity for a lifetime? The answer is to row like crazy. Take time for romantic activities. Think not of yourself but of the other. Avoid that which breeds conflict and resentment. And listen carefully to the needs of the partner. These are the keys to harmony and friendship.

It's difficult to keep two rowboats floating along together, but it can be done if each partner is determined to row. Unless they are willing to paddle, however, the currents of culture will separate them forever.

Defending the "Line of Respect"

One of the best ways to keep a marriage healthy is to maintain a system of mutual accountability within the context of love. This is done by protecting what I call the "line of respect" in a marital relationship. Let me illustrate.

Suppose I work in my office two hours longer than usual on a particular night, knowing that my wife, Shirley, is at home preparing a very special candlelight dinner. If I don't call to let her know I'll be late, you can bet that I'm going to hear about it when I get home. Shirley would see my behavior as insulting—and she'd be right. So she'd say, in effect, "Jim, what you did was selfish, and I can't let it pass." In those few words, and probably a few more, she would have spoken her mind in love and held me accountable for my disrespect. Then we would move on together.

In a healthy marriage, some things are worth defending, and mutual respect is at the top of the list. This doesn't mean you should nag, insult, publicly embarrass your mate, or point out insignificant indiscretions that should be overlooked. But a workable system of "checks and balances" can keep your marriage on course when issues of respect are at stake.

This kind of mutual accountability is the best way I know to avoid an unexpected explosion when stored resentment and anger reach a critical mass.

High-Voltage Marriages

Which of the following couples is more likely to enjoy the greatest physical attraction in their marriage? Is it the couple that spends every waking hour together and focuses almost exclusively on one another, or is it the man and woman who have other interests and then, after some time of independence, come closer together again as the pendulum swings?

Surprisingly, perhaps, it's the one that varies from time to time. According to behavioral researchers, the healthiest marriages and those with the highest sexual voltage are those that breathe—relationships that move from a time of closeness and tenderness to a more distant posture and then come together for another reunion as the cycle concludes.

This is why it's not always advantageous for a husband and wife to work together or to concentrate exclusively on one another in the absence of friends and colleagues outside the family. There is something about the diversity of interests and activities by each partner that keeps a couple from consuming one another and burning out the relationship in the short run.

Marriage is, after all, a marathon and not a sprint. Husbands and wives need to maintain a regenerating system that will keep love alive for a lifetime. Cultivating a healthy interest in many things is one big step in that direction.

Anticipating Life's Challenges

There are some facts of nature that never cease to astound me. For instance, did you know that before it snows, fir trees in northern regions actually retract their branches so that the weight of the snow they'll have to bear will be reduced? This withdrawal response is programmed into every branch, even in those smaller than a little finger. The Creator has enabled the tree to anticipate the problem before it occurs, thereby reducing the risks that might accompany a snowy winter.

Perhaps we can do something similar within our own marriages. You will not be able to avoid problems and crises in marriage, but you can anticipate them and prepare for their arrival. Most of the stress points in families are common to others and are therefore predictable.

One of my good friends spent a considerable amount of time with his wife preparing for the moment when their grown kids would move out of the house. They talked often about the empty nest and discussed ways their friends had coped with it. They read books about that phase of life and applied what they had heard to themselves. As a result, their transition to the empty nest was smooth and uneventful.

Into every marriage, a little snow will fall. Blizzards will blow, and storms will howl. But an effort to anticipate these difficult times will help you and your mate stand up under the weight of the winter storm.

Home Is Where the Heart Is

One thing that men need to understand is that, generally speaking, women tend to care more than men about the home and everything in it. It's certainly true in my house. Let me illustrate that point. A few years ago, my wife and I hired a plumber to install a gas-barbecue unit in the backyard, and then we left for the day. When we returned, we both observed that the device was mounted about eight inches too high.

Shirley and I stood looking at the appliance, and our reactions were quite different. I said, "Yeah, you're right. The plumber made a mistake. By the way, what are we having for dinner tonight?"

But Shirley reacted characteristically. She said, "I don't think I can stand that thing sticking up in the air like that."

I could have lived the rest of my life without thinking again about the height of the barbecue unit, but to Shirley it was a big deal. Why? Because to a man a home is a place where he can relax, kick off his shoes, and be himself. To a woman, especially a homemaker, the house is an extension of her personality. She expresses her individuality and her character through it. That's why husbands would be wise to recognize this differing perspective and accommodate the creative interests of their wives.

By the way, the plumber was summoned back to our house the next day and asked to fix his mistake. As the saying goes, "If Mama ain't happy, ain't nobody happy."

When Honesty Is Cruel

Most marriage counselors emphasize communication as the foundation for a healthy relationship—nothing should be withheld from the marital partner. There is wisdom in that advice, provided it is applied with common sense.

It's true that couples who communicate openly have a much better chance of succeeding in marriage. But any good idea can be misused—at which point the effect becomes negative. For example, it's honest for a man to tell his wife that he hates her fat legs, or her varicose veins, or the way she cooks. It's honest for a woman to dump her anger on her husband and constantly berate him for his shortcomings and his failures. But honesty that does not have the best interest of the other person at heart is really a cruel form of selfishness. This is especially true when the other person can't do anything about the characteristics that are being criticized.

Some couples, in their determination to share every thought and opinion, systematically destroy the sweet spark of romance that once drew them together. No longer is there any sense of mystique in the relationship. They've unraveled the romantic allure that made them love one another in the first place.

I'm not suggesting that husbands and wives begin to deceive each other. I am recommending, however, that they leave something to be discovered along the way and occasionally let their anger and frustration cool down just a bit before pouring it on an unsuspecting partner in the name of honesty.

The bottom line? Let love be your guide.

Legend of the Taj Mahal

The Taj Mahal is one of the most beautiful and costly tombs ever built, but there is something fascinating about its beginnings. In 1629, when the favorite wife of Indian ruler Shah Jahan died, he ordered that a magnificent tomb be built as a memorial to her. The shah placed his wife's casket in the middle of a parcel of land, and construction of the temple literally began around it. But several years into the venture, the Shah's grief for his wife gave way to a passion for the project. One day while he was surveying the site, he reportedly stumbled over a wooden box, and he had some workers throw it out. It was months before he realized that his wife's casket had been destroyed. The original purpose for the memorial became lost in the details of construction.[2]

This legend may or may not be true, but its theme is a familiar one in the lives of people. How many of us set out to build dream castles but lose our focus along the way? We realize too late that it is loved ones and our children that really matter.

Another classic example of misplaced values occurred in the life of J. Paul Getty, one of the richest men of the twentieth century. He wrote: "I've never been given to envy, save for the envy I feel toward those people who have the ability to make a marriage work and endure happily. It's an art I've never been able to master."[3]

While we're building our Taj Mahals, let's not forget the purpose with which we began building.[4]

After the Fight Is Over

I t's not the fights that should worry married couples; it's what happens when the battles are over.

Almost all husbands and wives experience conflict from time to time, which is not necessarily unhealthy to their relationships. A verbal spat that stays within reasonable limits can open the windows and give the couple a chance to vent frustrations and release some steam. The important question, however, is what happens after a fight is over? In healthy relationships, a period of confrontation ends in forgiveness, in drawing together, in deeper respect and understanding, and sometimes in sexual satisfaction. But in unstable marriages, conflict is never entirely resolved. This is a very dangerous situation, where the consequences of one battle begin to overlap with a prelude to the next. It's a good idea for couples to take a close look at what happens in the aftermath of confrontation.

Are there things that you've said or done that have grieved your partner? Do you need to ask forgiveness for attacking the self-worth of your spouse instead of focusing on the issues that divided you? Are there substantive matters that haven't yet been resolved? Deal with them quickly before they can fester and erode the relationship from within.

The apostle Paul understood this principle clearly. He instructed us not to let the sun go down on our wrath (Ephesians 4:26). That's great marital advice.

The Straight Life

I f we are to believe the findings of behavioral researchers, extramarital affairs are more common now than ever in the United States. People who ought to know better, such as ministers, physicians, and politicians, are risking marriages, careers, and children to engage in sexual misconduct. Even United States presidents have participated in one or more dalliances that have jeopardized their place in history. Immoral behavior of this nature is destroying millions of families at every level of society.

The question I would pose is this: What happens to individuals who cheat on their spouses—those who leave the "straight life" in pursuit of someone more exciting?

I have watched such people over the years, and what I've observed is that they eventually establish another "straight life." After the thrill of the chase and the cooling of passion, folks have to get back to cooking, cleaning, and earning a living. The grass is greener on the other side of the fence, but it still has to be mowed. Also, personal flaws and irritants show up, much like those in the former husband or wife. And guess what? The straight life begins to feel confining again. Then what does the individual do when he or she is beginning to feel trapped? Some people then hopscotch from one straight life to another in a vain search for something indescribable—something they never seem to find. Lying in their wake are former spouses, who feel rejected, bitter, and unloved. They produce vulnerable little children, who wonder why Daddy doesn't live here anymore and why Mommy cries all the time.

Soaps and sitcoms on television tell us every day that infidelity is a marvelous game for two. It sure does look like fun. But when adultery has run its course, it only brings pain and disillusionment. And the ones who are hurt the most are the children who are caught in the web.

Beating the Doldrums

Many marriages seem to lose the wind in their romantic sails and drift aimlessly through the sea of matrimony.

Their plight reminds me of seamen back in the days of wooden vessels. Sailors in that era had much to fear, including pirates, storms, and diseases. But their greatest fear was that the ship might encounter the doldrums. The doldrums was an area of the ocean near the equator characterized by calm and very light shifting winds. It could mean death for the entire crew. The ship's food and water supply would be exhausted as they drifted for days, or even weeks, waiting for a breeze to put them back on course.

Well, marriages that were once exciting and loving can also get caught in the romantic doldrums, causing the relationship to die a slow and painful death. Author Doug Fields, in his book *Creative Romance*, writes, "Dating and romancing your spouse can change those patterns, and it can be a lot of fun. There's no quick fix to a stagnant marriage, of course, but you can lay aside the excuses and begin to date your sweetheart again."

It'll take a conscious effort to fill your sail again, but some creative ideas will help. How about breakfast in bed? a kiss in the rain? or rereading those old love letters?

The honeymoon need not be a forgotten experience.

Mystery in Marriage

If you want to put some new life in your marriage, try thinking like a teenager again.

We all remember, fondly or otherwise, the craziness of our dating days. The coy attitudes, the flirting, the fantasies, the chasing after the prize. As we moved from courtship into marriage, most of us felt we should grow up and leave the game playing behind. But we may not have matured as much as we'd like to think.

In truth, our romantic relationships will always bear some characteristics of adolescent sexuality. Adults still love the thrill of the chase, the lure of the unattainable, the excitement of the new and boredom with the old. Immature impulses are controlled and minimized in a committed relationship, of course, but they never fully disappear.

This might be a key to keeping vitality in your marriage. If things seem stale between you and your spouse, maybe you should remember some old tricks. Maybe it's time for a little mystery, a little flirtatiousness, a date where you revisit the places you enjoyed when your love was new and relive some of the happy moments that brought you together.

If it sounds a little immature to act like a teenager again, just keep this in mind: In the best marriages, the chase is never really over.

For Better or for Worse

My friends Keith and Mary Korstjens have been married for more than fifty years. Shortly after their honeymoon, Mary was stricken with polio and became a quadriplegic. The doctors informed her that she would be confined to a wheelchair for the rest of her life. It was a devastating development, but Keith never wavered in his commitment to Mary. For all these years, he has bathed and dressed her, carried her to and from her bed, taken her to the bathroom, brushed her teeth, and combed her hair.

Obviously, Keith could have divorced Mary in 1957 and looked for a new and healthier wife, but he never even considered it. I admire this man, not only for doing the right thing, but for continuing to love and cherish his wife. Though the problems you and I face may be less challenging than those encountered by the Korstjens family, all of us will have our own difficulties. How will we respond? Some will give up on marriage for some pretty flimsy reasons. If we are going to go the distance, nothing short of an ironclad commitment will sustain us when the hard times come.

Let's review the vows spoken by millions during their marriage ceremonies. They read: "For better or for worse, for richer or for poorer, in sickness and in health, to love and to cherish, forsaking all others, from this day forward till death do us part." Keith and Mary Korstjens said and meant *exactly* that!

MONEY

Money Matters

Let's talk about money, which is the most common source of conflict in marriage. Money is divisive because men and women typically have very different ideas about how it ought to be used. My father, for example, was an avid hunter, and he thought nothing of buying three boxes of shotgun shells to use in an afternoon of recreational shooting. Yet if my mother, who loved to shop, spent an equal amount of money on an extra potato peeler, he considered it wasteful. Never mind that she enjoyed browsing in stores as much as he enjoyed traipsing through the fields. His values were simply different from hers.

Another disagreement about money involves the decision about when and for what credit should be obtained. This is dangerous territory for husbands and wives. Nothing irritates a disciplined, frugal person more than having a spouse who squanders their resources, and their future earnings, for things that aren't needed. These differences in perspective often surface during the honeymoon and become battlegrounds a few weeks later.

Accordingly, I'm convinced that the first principle of a healthy marriage is to stay out of debt and to be extremely careful with credit cards. Their misuse can undermine a family's financial stability, and they should be labeled "Danger! Handle with care!"

If money is a source of trouble in your family, sit down long enough to develop a plan on which you both agree, perhaps with the help of a financial counselor. It's the least you can do for one another.

The Millionaire

In the 1950s there was a popular television program called *The Millionaire* that featured a rich man who gave a million dollars anonymously each week to some unsuspecting person. Then we saw how the money changed the life of that individual. The outcome was always bad. Rather than solving problems or making life easier, the unexpected wealth just brought greed, violence, and conflict.

Well, that was just fiction—or was it? The truth is that sudden wealth often has precisely that effect on those who achieve it. With the spread of state lotteries throughout the United States, there are numerous new millionaires each year. We're seeing now what happens to those "lucky" people who hold the winning tickets.

Would you believe that one-third of all lottery winners go from rags to riches—to bankruptcy? And another 25 percent wind up selling the remaining payments at a discounted rate to pay off debts. A company that buys those future payments already holds $500 million in face-value jackpots. The CEO, Richard Salvato, said, "The trouble with getting all that money is that it amplifies the person's weaknesses. If they were reckless with their ordinary paychecks, they're also reckless with the bigger ones. People just don't change."[1]

So if you're fantasizing about winning the lottery and living on easy street for the rest of your life, it's probably a pipe dream. First, your chances of hitting the jackpot are infinitesimal, and second, even if you do—your troubles are just beginning. I learned that from *The Millionaire* in 1955.

Rich Kids

Demographers and attorneys tell us that something dramatic is happening to the baby-boomer generation, which is now averaging nearly sixty years of age. They will soon inherit more than $10.4 trillion as their parents pass from the scene. It will be the greatest transfer of wealth in the history of the world.[2] The question is, how will they handle this sudden affluence?

There may be a clue in a sociological study reported in a book by John Sedgwick called *Rich Kids*. The author made an extensive investigation of those who inherit large trust funds. He concluded that sudden wealth can be dangerous. For some, not having to work can lead to irresponsible living and addictive behavior, such as gambling and alcoholism. Money can also tear marriages to threads. Finally, absolutely nothing will divide siblings quicker than money, setting up fights over family businesses and resentment of those designated to run them.[3]

There are exceptions to these negative consequences, of course. Some people handle wealth and power gracefully. But it is a risky passage at best and one that requires a great deal of maturity and self-control. At the least, wealthy parents should ask themselves some important questions, especially if their heirs are young. Should they remove the very challenges that helped Mom and Dad succeed in the early days—the obligation to work hard, live frugally, save, build, and produce by the sweat of their brows? And even if their sons and daughters *are* able to handle a generous inheritance, how will their grandchildren and future generations respond?

I know my views on this subject are unconventional. One of the reasons people work hard is so their children and future heirs won't have to. They love their kids and want to make things easier for them. Even so, giving a large trust fund to those who don't earn it should be done only with the greatest care and preparation.

It takes a steady hand to hold a full cup!

Home Business

For many families an appealing way to bring extra income into the home is by building a home-based business. Is it possible to work out of your home while still taking care of your children and other duties—and without losing your mind? The answer is yes.

Everything from catering, desktop publishing, pet grooming, sewing, consulting, transcribing legal documents, or even mail-order sales can be done at home. Choosing which business is right for you is the first of three practical steps suggested by Donna Partow, author of a book called *Homemade Business.*[4]

Donna said you can start your own enterprise by taking a personal skills and interest inventory to identify your particular abilities and what you might like doing best. The second step is to do your homework. Begin by asking your librarian to help you research your chosen field. Look up books, magazines, and newspaper articles. Talk to other people who have done what you would most like to do. Join an industry organization and a network. Subscribe to relevant publications.

According to Mrs. Partow, the third step is to marshal as much support as you can. Get your children, your spouse, and friends on your side. Setting up a small business can be stressful, and you'll need as much encouragement as you can get.

If you've been torn between family and finances, having a home-based business may turn out to provide for you and your family the best of both worlds.

How Much Is Enough?

We were talking earlier about lottery winners and what happens to those who become sudden millionaires. Follow-up studies confirm that one-third of the sudden millionaires are bankrupt within a few years. Some lose their fortunes to bad business deals, extravagant living, crazy schemes, and fast-talking relatives. They simply lack the ability to handle money—especially huge amounts of it.

But there is another great threat to unearned riches. It is likely that many of the big winners continue to gamble as before, only this time with much bigger stakes. Having won against impossible odds only convinces them that they are charmed in some way. After all, lady luck was generous last time—why not again? It would be fascinating to know how commonly multimillion-dollar purses are quickly squandered in subsequent gambling pursuits. Unfortunately, few are willing to admit it.

There's an important principle here for all of us—not just those who win jackpots. Unless you spend less than you earn, no amount of income will be enough. That's why some people get salary increases and then slide even deeper into debt. Let me say it again: No amount of income will be sufficient if spending is not brought under control. The only way to get ahead financially is to deny ourselves some of the things we want. If we don't have the discipline to do that, we will always be in debt.

Consider the finances of the United States government. It extracts more than a trillion dollars annually from American taxpayers. That's a thousand billion bucks! But in recent years our Congress outspent that enormous income by $5.6 trillion, increasing the debt by a billion dollars every thirty-two hours.[5]

The point is inescapable: Whether it be within a government or by a private individual, we have to be willing to live within our means. If we won't do that, then not even a fifteen-million-dollar jackpot will save us.

Easy come, easy go, as they say.

MOTHERHOOD

Dad as the Interpreter of Mom

Where do children learn to think highly of their mothers? Who sets the pattern for their young minds, positioning Mom as a much-loved and respected member of the family—instead of being chief cook and scrub lady?

The best public-relations agent for Mom—is Dad. Fathers can wield tremendous influence over what children think of their mothers, or of women in general. Early in my marriage to Shirley, I learned that occasional irritation between us quickly reflected itself in the behavior of our children. They seemed to feel, "If Dad can argue with Mom, then we can, too." I learned how important it was to express love and admiration for my wife, even when there were issues that we needed to iron out beyond their gaze. In short, my attitudes became the attitudes of my children, which I now know to be typical.

In a world that often discounts the contribution of women, especially homemakers, it's up to us as husbands to say in a dozen ways, "Your mother is a wonderful woman! She works hard and she deserves tremendous credit for what she gives to us all. As far as I'm concerned, she's number one!"

Kids will quickly recognize the respect shown by a father and reflect it in their attitudes and behavior. It is a public-relations assignment that only dads can perform.

It's All Hard Work

When I hear someone comment that being a mother and home-maker is boring, I have a simple response: You could be right!

The truth is, almost any occupation you can name—from a telephone operator to a medical pathologist to an attorney or a dentist—involves long hours of tedious activity. Few of us enjoy heart-thumping excitement each moment of our professional lives. I once stayed in a hotel right next to the room of a famous cellist who was performing in a classical concert that evening. I could hear him through the walls as he practiced hour after hour. He didn't play beautiful symphonic renditions; he repeated scales and runs and exercises, over and over and over. Believe me! This practice began early in the morning and continued until the time of his concert. As he strolled onto the stage that night, I'm sure many in the audience thought to themselves, *What a glamorous life!* Some glamour! I happen to know he spent the entire day in his lonely hotel room in the company of his cello.

No, I doubt if the job of being a mother and homemaker is more boring than most other jobs, particularly if a woman refuses to be isolated from adult contact. But regarding the importance of the assignment, no job can compete with the satisfaction of shaping and molding and guiding a new human being.

Mom as the Interpreter of Dad

Is Dad thought of as a hero or a bum in his home? The answer probably depends on what Mom thinks.

This maternal influence is powerfully expressed in the book *Fathers and Sons,* by Lewis Yablonsky. He told about sitting around the dinner table listening to his mother say things like, "Look at your father! His shoulders are bent down; he's a failure. He doesn't have the courage to get a better job or make more money. He's a beaten man."

Yablonsky's father never defended himself. He just kept staring at his plate. As a result, his three sons grew up believing their father really was a wimp. They never noticed his virtues or the fact that he did indeed work hard to support his family.

Yablonsky concluded with this statement: "My overall research clearly supports that the mother is the basic filter and has enormous significance on the father-son relationship." I strongly agree. How much better for a wife to praise her husband, to point out his strengths, to position him in the children's eyes as someone with courage and principles.

Mom's going to need the influence of a strong man in the lives of her children. She would do well to contribute to their image of him as a leader.

In Recognition of Mothers

My commentary on this occasion is in honor of mothers around the world. There is no assignment on earth that requires the array of skills and understanding needed by a mom in fulfilling her everyday duties. She must be a resident psychologist, physician, theologian, educator, nurse, chef, taxi driver, fire marshal, and occasional police officer.

Join her on a midmorning visit to the pediatrician's office. After sitting for forty-five minutes with a cranky, feverish toddler on her lap, Mom and baby are finally ushered into the examining room. The doctor checks out the sick child and then tells the woman with a straight face, "Be sure you keep him quiet for four or five days. Don't let him scratch the rash. Make certain he keeps the medicine down, and you'll want to watch his stools."

"Yeah sure, Doc! Any other suggestions?"

"Just one. This disease is contagious. Keep your other four kids away from him. I'll see you in a week."

The amazing thing is that most mothers would get this job done—and they'd do it with love and wisdom. God made 'em good at what they do. And He gave them a passion for their children. They would, quite literally, lay down their lives to protect the kids entrusted to their care. And that's why they are deserving of our admiration—on Mother's Day, or on any other day of the year.

Combating "Soul Hunger"

Women who feel isolated and lonely often look to their husbands to satisfy what has been called their "soul hunger." It is a role men have never handled very well. I doubt if farmers came in from the fields one hundred years ago to have heart-to-heart talks with their wives.

What *has* changed in that time is the relationship between women. A century ago, great support and camaraderie existed between wives and mothers. They cooked together, went to church together, and grew old together. And when a baby was born, aunts, grandmothers, and neighbors were there to show the new mother how to diaper, feed, and discipline.

Today, however, the extended family has all but disappeared, depriving women of that traditional source of support. Furthermore, American families move every three or four years, preventing long-term friendships from developing.

It's also important for women to understand that some of their needs simply can't be met by men.

In the classic book *Anne of Green Gables* by Lucy M. Montgomery, there's a wonderful moment when the teenage Anne says, "A bosom friend—an intimate friend, you know—a really kindred spirit to whom I can confide my inmost soul. I've dreamed of meeting her all my life." She expresses a longing that is common to women, but not so typical in men. It's the need for intimate friendship. I think this is a key to understanding the incidence of depression common among many women today.

To combat this sense of isolation, it is extremely important for women to maintain a network of friends through exercise classes, group hobbies, church activities, or bicycle clubs. The interchange between them may sound like casual talk, but the bonding that occurs there makes life a lot more satisfying.

Maintaining a Reserve Army

A good military general will never commit all of his soldiers to the battlefield at the same time. He keeps a reserve force to relieve exhausted soldiers when they stagger back from the front lines. Parents of teenagers would do well to follow the same strategy. Let me explain.

It is common today for mothers of preschoolers to believe that the heavy demands of raising children will diminish once their kids reach school age. Then, she thinks, she can accept a heavier workload and other activities without sacrificing the needs of her children. It is my belief that the teenage years often generate more pressure and make greater demands on parents than when their kids are small. Besides the common rebellion of those years, there's the chauffeuring, the supervising, the cooking and cleaning, the noise and chaos that surround an ambitious teenager. Someone in the family must be available to respond to these challenges and the other stresses associated with adolescence.

It's a wise parent, then, who takes care not to exhaust himself or herself when so much is going on at home. A reservoir of energy is needed to deal with the unexpected and the difficult. To the degree possible, keep the family schedule simple, get plenty of rest, eat nutritious meals, and prepare to deal competently with the challenges of those years.

This is why I believe, though many will disagree, that it is as important for mothers of teenagers to be at home as it is for those raising preschoolers. That's the best way to maintain a reserve army when it's needed most.

Full-Time Mothers

Let me ask, do you think it is appropriate for a woman, especially a college student, to make it her exclusive career goal to be a wife and mother? Or is that a waste of her talents? Most women's studies programs in large universities consider the choice of homemaking to be almost a betrayal.

I remember a senior who came to ask me about that issue. We talked about various job opportunities and the possibility of her going to graduate school. Then she suddenly paused, leaned toward me, and said almost in a whisper, "May I be completely honest with you?"

I said, "Sure, Julie. There's no one here but us. You can say anything you want."

"Well," she said in a hushed tone, "I don't want to have a career at all. What I really want is to be a full-time wife and mother."

I asked, "Why do you say it as though it's some kind of secret? It's your life. What's wrong with doing whatever you want?"

"Are you kidding?" she replied. "If my professors and my classmates at the university knew that's what I wanted, they'd laugh me out of school."

How unfortunate that a young woman should have to apologize for wanting to have babies and devote herself to their care for a few years. That way of life has been honored and respected for centuries, yet it has fallen into disrepute.

Not every woman chooses to be a full-time homemaker, of course. Some are more interested in a career, and that is certainly their prerogative. Others have no plans to marry. That's all right, too. But those who *do* elect to be stay-at-home moms should not be ashamed to admit it—even on a university campus.

Oh yes, and what about Julie? She has three beautiful teenagers now and still loves her job as a full-time mom. And why not, for Pete's sake?

PARENTING

Sending the Roots Down Deep

Contrary to what some parents may believe, the ideal environment for a child is not one devoid of problems and trials.

Though it's hard to accept at the time, your children need the minor setbacks and disappointments that come their way. How can they learn to cope with problems and frustrations if their early experiences are totally without trial? Nature tells us so. A tree that's planted in a rain forest is never forced to extend its roots downward in search of water. Consequently, it remains poorly anchored and can be toppled by even a moderate wind. By contrast, a mesquite tree that's planted in a dry desert is threatened by its hostile environment. It can only survive by sending its roots down thirty feet or more into the earth, seeking cool water. But through this adaptation to an arid land, the well-rooted tree becomes strong and steady against all assailants.

Our children are like the two trees in some ways. Those who have learned to conquer their problems are better anchored than those who have never faced them.

Our task as parents, then, is not to eliminate every challenge for our children. Rather, it is to serve as a confident ally on their behalf, encouraging them when they're distressed, intervening when the threats become overwhelming, and "being there" when the crises come. Above all, we need to give them the tools with which to overcome the inevitable obstacles of life.

How Tough Is Parenting?

A few years ago I asked one thousand mothers and fathers to describe their greatest frustrations in raising kids. I heard many humorous stories in response about sticky telephones and wet toilet seats and knotted shoestrings. One mother actually wanted to know why toddlers never throw up in the bathroom. To do so would violate an unwritten law of the universe, to be sure.

But in our poll, parents didn't merely laugh about their frustrations—they tended to blame themselves. They said they were overwhelmed and were losing confidence in their ability to do the job. Many were having trouble just coping from day to day. How sad it is that this ancient responsibility of raising children has become so burdensome and laden with guilt.

Actually, the facts won't support that self-condemnation in the majority of cases. Most moms and dads are doing a credible job at home. And it's time that someone patted them on the back for their commitment and their sacrifice. And someday, when the frustrations of toddlerhood and the turmoil of adolescence have passed, they'll enjoy the sweet benefits of being very good and loving parents.

Hang in there, moms and dads. You're more skilled than you think you are.

Busy Fathers and Exhausted Mothers

I spoke at a White House conference a few years ago during which the other speaker was Dr. Armand Nicholi, a psychiatrist from Harvard University. His topic, like mine, was the status of the American family.

Dr. Nicholi explained how an overcommitted lifestyle that makes parents inaccessible to their children produces much the same effect as divorce itself, and herein lies our most serious failing as mothers and fathers. Cross-cultural studies make it clear that parents in the United States spend less time with their children than parents in almost any other nation in the world. For decades, fathers have devoted themselves exclusively to their occupations and activities away from home. More recently, mothers have joined the workforce in huge numbers, rendering themselves exhausted at night and burdened with domestic duties on weekends. The result: No one is at home to meet the needs of lonely preschoolers and latchkey children. Dr. Nicholi expressed regret that his comments would make many parents feel uncomfortable and guilty. However, he felt obligated to report the facts as he saw them.

Most important, Dr. Nicholi stressed as the point of his address the undeniable link between the interruption of parent-child relationships and the escalation of psychiatric problems that we were then seeing. If the trend continued, he said, serious national health problems were inevitable. One-half of all hospital beds in the United States at that time were taken up by psychiatric patients. That figure could hit 95 percent if the incidence of divorce, child abuse, child molestation, and child neglect continues to soar. In that event, we'll also see vast increases in teen suicide, already up more than 300 percent in twenty-five years, and drug abuse, crimes of violence, and problems related to sexual disorientation.

A Word About Parental Guilt

In case you haven't noticed, parenthood is a very guilt-producing endeavor, even for the dedicated professional.

Since there's no such creature as a perfect parent, we subject ourselves to a constant cross-examination in the courtroom of parental acceptability. Was my discipline fair? Did I overreact out of frustration and anger? Have I been partial to the child who's my secret favorite? Have I made the same mistakes for which I resented my own parents? Round and round go the self-doubts and recriminations, and guilt becomes a constant companion, especially for those whose kids are grown and whose record is already in the books.

The best way to handle parental guilt is to face it squarely, using it as a source of motivation for change where it's warranted. I would suggest that mothers and fathers sit down together and discuss their feelings. Write down the most troubling shortcomings. Then ask, "Is our guilt valid? Can we do anything about it? If so, what? If not, isn't it appropriate that we lay the matter to rest?"

Remember that we can no more be perfect parents than we can be perfect human beings. We get tired, frustrated, disappointed, and irritable, which necessarily affects the way we approach those little ones around our feet. Fortunately, we are permitted to make many mistakes through the years, provided the overall tone is somewhere near the right note.

Peace in the Neighborhood

Is there anything parents can do about the misbehavior of other parents' children in a neighborhood? As a matter of fact, there is.

They can bring about a more peaceful atmosphere on their street if they will simply talk to each other—but that can take some doing. There is no quicker way to anger a mama bear than for someone to criticize her precious cub. That's a delicate subject indeed. And that's why the typical neighborhood provides very little feedback to parents in regard to the behavior of their children. The kids know there are no lines of communication between adults, and they take advantage of the barrier.

What each block needs is a mother or father who has the courage to say, "I want to be told what my child does when he's beyond his own yard. If he's a brat with other children, I would like to know it. If he's disrespectful with adults, please mention it to me. I won't consider it tattling. I won't resent your coming to me. I hope I can share my insights regarding your children, too."

As tough as it is to hear that our kids have misbehaved, because it makes us feel like bad parents, we should open ourselves to that information if it's valid. None of our kids is perfect. We'll know better how to teach and discipline them if we talk openly and honestly to each of our neighbors as adults and friends.

Compulsive Parenting

I have expressed concern for years about absentee parents who regularly neglect their children during the developmental years. This problem continues in the fast-paced culture in which we live. But there are other parents—although fewer in number—at the other end of the continuum. It is prevalent among mothers, in particular, who become obsessed by their children. Their responsibilities leave no time for recreational, romantic, or restful activities. And not even Mother Teresa would have qualified as a babysitter.

Now, I don't question the motives of obsessive parents, but their preoccupation can lead to serious problems. First, making children the centerpiece of life is not in their best interests. It can lead in some cases to overprotection, permissiveness, and dependency.

Second, emotional and physical fatigue produce what is known as *parental burnout.* Just as a battery cannot continually be drained, the human body must be recharged from time to time. Burnout is destructive to the entire family, especially to the children for whom the effort was intended in the first place.

Third, superparenting can also be destructive to a marriage, especially when the mother is the one so inclined. A father may come to resent the children for taking his wife away from him, or she may think her husband is selfish because he won't match her commitment. Either way, a wedge is driven between them that could eventually destroy the family.

It is a pattern that is more common than you might think. Moderation is the key to healthy family life—even in one's approach to parenting.

Avoiding Revolution at Home

One of the most difficult parenting responsibilities involves the orderly transfer of power to our children. A common mistake is to grant autonomy before kids are really ready to handle it. That can be a disaster for immature and impulsive offspring. But it's just as dangerous to retain parental power too long. Control will be torn from our grasp if we refuse to surrender it voluntarily.

Consider, for example, how England treated her children in the American colonies. The early settlers left the mother country and grew to become rebellious teenagers who demanded their freedom. Still, the British refused to release them, and much unnecessary bloodshed resulted. England learned a valuable lesson from that painful experience, however, and 171 years later she granted a peaceful and orderly transfer of power to another tempestuous offspring named India. Revolution was averted.

With regard to our children, the granting of self-determination must be matched stride-for-stride with the arrival of maturity, culminating with complete release during early adulthood. But the task isn't as easy as it sounds. The key is to chart a path between the two extremes of letting go too early and hanging on too long. Only great tact, wisdom, and prayer will help us determine the timing of that difficult decision.

The Window of Opportunity

There are some skills that can be learned during the early childhood years that become very difficult to teach later on. For example, have you ever wondered why it's so easy for preschoolers to learn any language they hear? Russian, Chinese, Spanish, Hebrew—it really doesn't matter. Children can learn it perfectly without even a trace of an accent. Yet fifteen or twenty years later, most individuals will have a much harder time trying to make those same sounds.

Researchers now know why this is true. It's explained by a process known as "phoneme contraction." You see, the larynx of a young child assumes a shape necessary to make any sounds that he's learning to use at that time. It then solidifies or hardens in those positions, making it impossible or very difficult to make other sounds later in life. In other words, there's a window of opportunity when anything is possible linguistically, but it closes very quickly.

A child's attitude toward parental leadership is also like that. He or she passes through a brief period during toddlerhood and the preschool years when respect for authority and a certain sense of awe can be instilled. But that window closes very quickly. That's why it's so important to "shape the will" during the early years by balancing unconditional love with consistent firmness at home.

If parents miss that opportunity, the adolescent years can be bumpier than they need to be.

Beating Burnout

I talk to many mothers these days, especially those with younger kids, who feel like they're on the edge of burnout. They feel like they will explode if they have to do one more load of laundry or tie one more shoe. Their circumstances are very different from those of their grandmothers, who typically had extended families and neighbors to help them raise their kids. They were surrounded by mothers, aunts, sisters, and friends who provided encouragement, advice, and support in times of need.

But in today's mobile, highly energized society, young mothers are much more isolated and lonely. Many of them hardly know the women next door, and their sisters and mothers may live a thousand miles away. That's why it is so important for those with small children to stay in touch with the outside world. Though it may seem safer and less taxing to remain cloistered within the four walls of a home, it is a mistake to do so. Loneliness does bad things to the mind. Furthermore, there are many ways to network with other women today, including church activities, Bible study groups, and support programs, such as Moms In Prayer International and Mothers of Preschoolers.

Husbands of stay-at-home mothers need to recognize the importance of their support, too. It is a wise man who plans a romantic date at least once a week and occasionally offers to take care of the children so Mom can get a much-needed break.

In short, burnout is not inevitable even in a busy household. It can be avoided in families that recognize its symptoms and take steps to head it off.

Carving the Stone

Smithsonian magazine once featured a master stonecutter from England named Simon Verity, a man who honed his craft by restoring thirteenth-century cathedrals in Great Britain.

As the authors watched him work, they noticed something very interesting. They wrote, "Verity listens closely to hear the song of the stone under his careful blows. A solid strike, and all is well. A higher-pitched ping, and it could mean trouble. A chunk of rock could break off. He constantly adjusts the angle of the chisel and the force of the mallet to the pitch, pausing frequently to run his hand over the freshly carved surface."[1]

Verity understood the importance of his task. He knew that one wrong move could be devastating, causing irreparable damage to his work of art. His success was rooted in his ability to read the signals his stones were sending.

In similar fashion, parents need to hone their skills at listening to their children, especially during times of discipline and guidance. It takes a great deal of patience and sensitivity to interpret the child's responses. If you listen carefully, your boys and girls will tell you what they're thinking and feeling.

So whether shaping a child's character or sculpting in stone, the skills needed are crucial to a successful outcome. The honing by the master carver will create a beautiful work of art.

The Longest Task

Have you ever considered how long it takes to raise a human being from birth to maturity and get him or her ready for independent living?

Other creatures do the job much more quickly. Hamsters are ready to go on their own in three weeks. Kittens require only a couple of months, and lion cubs are self-sufficient within two years. Meanwhile, it takes twenty years or more to produce a son or daughter who can earn a living, stay out of trouble, and make normal adult decisions.

Noted author Elisabeth Elliot has written: "There never has been a time when children could successfully be raised without sacrifice and discipline on the part of the parents."[2] There simply aren't any shortcuts or easy ways to do the job right. Let's face it—the child-rearing task is the most protracted responsibility we are likely to face. And like any other project worth doing, the important thing is to persevere to the finish line.

Why have I offered this advice today? Because there are many voices out there telling parents to give up, to bail out, to think only of themselves. And there will be many discouraging moments along the way. But as the father of two grown kids, I can tell you that the child-rearing task is worth what it costs us—right through to its conclusion.

The Empty Nest

Several years ago, our youngest child, Ryan, went off to Chicago for his freshman year of college. His final day at home was filled with the hustle and bustle of packing and getting ready for a new life. Somehow amid all that activity, the gravity of the evening was missed. But then as we were driving him to the airport the next morning, it dawned on me that parenthood was over. An unexpected wave of grief swept over me. I thought I couldn't stand to see Ryan leave. It wasn't that I wanted to hold him in childhood or to exercise control of his life. No, I mourned the end of an era—a precious time of my life when Ryan and his sister, Danae, were young and their voices rang in the halls of our house. I couldn't hide the tears as we hugged good-bye at gate 18.

If you're thinking that I'm hopelessly sentimental about my kids, you're right. But I hope my experience encourages those of you whose children are still underfoot. The days that you've been given to care for them are much briefer than you think. Yes, it's a difficult and exhausting assignment, but I urge you to stay the course and finish the job.

By the way, about a month after the departure of our youngest, the empty nest began to look very different to us. The house stayed clean longer, our lives were definitely more tranquil, and my wife and I had more time to enjoy each other. I was reminded of the words of King Solomon, who wrote, "There is a time for everything, and a season for every activity under the heavens" (Ecclesiastes 3:1). That is even true for the task of raising children, and for us, that season has passed.

But if you happen to see my son or daughter, ask them to call home, won't you?

PARENTING CHILDREN

The Nurturance of Babies

In the thirteenth century, King Frederick II conducted an experiment with fifty infants to determine what language they would speak if never permitted to hear the spoken word. So he assigned foster mothers to bathe and suckle the children but forbade them to fondle, pet, or talk to their charges. The experiment failed because all fifty infants died. We learned hundreds of years later that babies who aren't touched and cuddled often fail to thrive.

The world has recently been exposed to yet another example of neglected and abused children. Mary Carlson, a researcher from Harvard Medical School, observed an overcrowded Romanian orphanage, where row upon row of babies lay neglected in their cribs. The staff was hopelessly overworked, so the babies were rarely touched even at mealtime. What struck Carlson was the silence in the nursery. There was no crying, no babbling, not even a whimper. Upon physical examinations given at age two, Carlson found that the babies had unusually high amounts of a stress hormone in the blood called cortisol, which is known to damage the brain. Growth was stunted, and the children acted half their age.[1]

It isn't sufficient to feed, clothe, and care for the physical needs of children. It is now clear that touching and nurturance are critical to their survival.

Babies Are Listening

B e careful what you say in the presence of your babies. That's the advice of a researcher at Johns Hopkins University, who tells us that children only eight months of age are capable of hearing and remembering words, good or bad.

"Little ears are listening," says Dr. Peter Juscyzk. Babies in this study, which appears in the prestigious journal *Science,* were exposed to three recorded stories for a period of about ten days. Two weeks later they were tested in the lab and clearly recognized the words in the stories, while failing to respond to those they hadn't heard. Robin Chapman, a language specialist at the University of Wisconsin, emphasized the importance of this study. It demonstrates that very young children do attend to the sounds of language and are able to pick out those that are familiar.

"These findings are significant to parents because they tell us that reading to children at an early age can be beneficial to language development, even if they don't appear to comprehend. Reading also starts the process of learning how words are formed and used. It helps babies segment sounds out of speech," said Dr. Juscyzk.[2]

Finally, the study shows, according to Chapman, that "a lot of language learning is happening in the first year of life. It shows that parents should talk to their children and that children will learn about language from that talk."[3]

Interesting stuff—but mothers have known it intuitively for five thousand years!

Sudden Infant Death Syndrome

You've probably heard about the tragic phenomenon known as sudden infant death syndrome, or SIDS. It's still claiming the lives of about six thousand babies each year in the United States alone.[4]

This killer has mystified medical researchers. Now a study conducted by the U.S. Consumer Product Safety Commission, in collaboration with researchers at the University of Maryland and Washington University–St. Louis, has shed light on the issue. The epidemiologist who directed the investigation, Dr. N.J. Shear, said: "We have not found a cause for SIDS, but our results show that specific items of bedding used in the U.S., such as comforters and pillows, were associated with an increased risk for death to prone sleeping infants whose faces became covered."

This means that babies should not be placed on their stomachs in soft bedding. That precaution will lessen the likelihood that they will rebreathe their own carbon dioxide that's trapped in the blankets and pillows around them. In about 30 percent of the 206 SIDS deaths in the research project, babies were found with bedding pressed against their noses and mouths. The advice now being offered by doctors is that parents place their infants on their backs, not on their stomachs, and that a minimum amount of loose bedding be kept in the crib.[5]

This advice won't eliminate all cases of SIDS, but it could save hundreds, if not thousands, of lives every year.

Building Confidence in the Preteen

If confidence is something we value for our sons and daughters, maybe it would be helpful to assist them in achieving it.

Today it seems like every teenager has to come along and bump his or her head on the same old rock, experiencing those terrible feelings of inadequacy and inferiority. To help kids minimize that experience, I've found it beneficial to talk to them about confidence long before adolescence has arrived.

For example, when your child meets another boy or girl who's very shy, you might say afterward, "Did you notice that Pam didn't look at anyone when she spoke? Why do you suppose she seemed so embarrassed and uncomfortable? Do you think it's because she doesn't have much confidence in herself?"

Then in the period immediately before puberty, make it known that the teen years are often accompanied by a massive assault on self-worth, where everybody seems to feel ugly and unintelligent and useless. But also explain that this is a temporary experience, like going through a tunnel from which you will inevitably emerge. It would also be wise in this twilight of childhood to discuss the sexual awakening that's about to occur, including how the body will change and how to use this new experience responsibly and morally. To not do so is to leave the child to cope alone with the terrors of menstruation or other physical transformations.

So much can be done to prepare kids for the coming crises in adolescence if we'll give a little thought to the task.

Preparing for Adolescence

A parent who sees the unmistakable signs of adolescence beginning to arrive in a son or daughter needs to set aside some time for a final all-important conversation.

In many ways, the parent of a preteen has a task similar to a football coach who has trained his squad all through the late summer and early fall. Finally the first game is about to occur, when direct coaching is not going to be possible. He gathers the kids in the locker room and makes one last speech before they take the field. He reminds them of the fundamentals and gives them the old pep talk about winning.

In a similar way, parents of preteens have been teaching their youngsters all through preschool and the elementary years. They've been teaching about right and wrong, what they believe, and how to behave. There's so much that they need to summarize in this pep talk. Soon the big contest called adolescence will begin and the teen will take the field. From that point forward, very little parental advice can be given.

That's why I recommend that parents take an eleven- or twelve-year-old child on a "preparing for adolescence" trip, during which moral values and the family's principles are repeated and emphasized. Sex education and the physical changes of adolescence, the approaching social pressures, and other fundamentals should be discussed.

That conversation should end with a Knute Rockne inspirational message—giving them a loving hug and sending the team onto the field. Then hold your breath and pray like crazy.

Of Balloons and Children

Several years ago I attended a wedding ceremony in a beautiful garden setting, and I came away with some thoughts on child rearing.

After the minister had instructed the groom to kiss the bride on that day, approximately one hundred and fifty colorful, helium-filled balloons were released into the blue California sky. Within a few seconds the balloons were scattered all across the heavens, some of them rising hundreds of feet overhead and others cruising toward the horizon. A few balloons struggled to clear the upper branches of the trees while the show-offs became mere pinpoints of color on their journey across the sky.

How interesting, I thought, and how symbolic of children. Let's face it—some boys and girls seem to be born with more helium than others. They catch all the right breezes, and they soar effortlessly to the heights, while others wobble dangerously close to the trees. Their frantic folks run along underneath, huffing and puffing to keep them airborne. It is an exhausting experience.

I want to offer a word of encouragement specifically to the parents of those low-flying kids. Sometimes the child who has the greatest trouble getting off the ground eventually soars to the highest heights. That's why I urge you as parents not to look too quickly for the person your child will become.

The Antecedents of Disease

We've discussed the incredible vulnerability of infants and toddlers. Many investigations in recent years have confirmed that touch and emotional nurturance in the first few years of life are necessary to survival.

Now, a study conducted at Harvard University shows unmistakably that the quality of the bonding between a boy and his mother is related to his physical health forty or fifty years later. Remarkably, 91 percent of college men who said they had not enjoyed a close relationship with their mothers developed coronary artery disease, hypertension, duodenal ulcers, or alcoholism by the midlife years. Only 45 percent of the men who recalled maternal warmth and closeness had similar illnesses. The same was true of men and relationships with their fathers. And consider this: 100 percent of participants in this study whose mothers and fathers were cold and distant suffered numerous diagnosed diseases in midlife.

In short, the quality of early relationships between boys and their parents is a powerful predictor of lifelong health. And you can be sure, the same is true of girls and women.

It comes down to this: When early needs are not met, trouble looms down the road.[6]

The Hurried Child

There is a tendency for parents in Western nations to make their children grow up too quickly, rushing them through the milestones of childhood and propelling them into the pressures of adolescence. This is the conclusion of developmental psychologist Dr. David Elkind, who called this cultural phenomenon the "Hurried Child Syndrome." It occurs when parents encourage their children to behave like teenagers, such as buying makeup for preschool girls, permitting teenage dating, treating kids more like grown-ups, expecting them to make adult-level decisions, dressing them in designer clothes, and especially, exposing them to explicit sexuality in movies, television, and music videos.[7]

In years past, parents understood the need for an orderly progression through childhood. There were cultural "markers" that determined the ages at which certain behaviors were appropriate. Boys, for example, wore short pants until they were twelve or thirteen. Those markers have disappeared, or they've been moved downward. It was a big mistake.

When you treat your children as if they're grown, it becomes very difficult to set limits on their adolescent behavior down the road. How can you establish a curfew for a thirteen-year-old, for example, who has been taught to think of himself or herself as an adult?

In short, the "Hurried Child Syndrome" robs our kids of childhood and places them on an unnatural timetable that's harmful to mental and physical health. Let's let our kids be kids.

Ordinary Kids

When the birth of a firstborn child is imminent, his parents pray that he will be normal; that is, average. But from that moment on, average will not be good enough.

Their child must excel. He must succeed. He must triumph. He must be the first of his age to walk or talk or ride a tricycle. He must earn a stunning report card and amaze his teachers with his wit and wisdom. He must star in Little League, and later he must be quarterback or senior class president or valedictorian. His sister must be the cheerleader or the soloist or the homecoming queen. Throughout the formative years of childhood, his parents give him the same message day after day: "We're counting on you to do something fantastic, Son. Now don't disappoint us."

Unfortunately, exceptional children are just that...exceptions. Seldom does a five-year-old memorize the King James Version of the Bible, or play chess blindfolded, or compose symphonies in the Mozart manner. To the contrary, the vast majority of our children are not dazzlingly brilliant, extremely witty, highly coordinated, tremendously talented, or universally popular. They are just plain kids with oversized needs to be loved and accepted as they are.

Most parents have average kids, and to expect more sets the stage for considerable disappointment for parents and puts unrealistic pressure on the younger generation.

Maximizing Your Child's Potential

According to a ten-year study conducted by Dr. Burton White and a team of researchers at Harvard University, there are six factors that are related to the eventual intellectual capacity of a child:

1. The most critical period for the child's mental development is between eight and eighteen months of age.

2. The mother is the most important person in the child's environment.

3. The amount of "live" language directed to the child between twelve and fifteen months is absolutely crucial.

4. Those children who are given free access to living areas of their homes progressed much faster than those whose movements are restricted.

5. The nuclear family is the most important educational delivery system.

6. The best parents are those who excel at three key functions: They are superb designers and organizers of their children's environments; they permit their children to interrupt them for brief thirty-second episodes, during which personal comfort and information are exchanged; finally, they are firm disciplinarians while simultaneously showing great affection for their children.[8]

In other words, this ten-year investigation conducted by learned researchers revealed precisely what most mothers have always known they should do: Love their kids, talk to them, treat them with respect, expose them to interesting things, organize their time, discipline them fairly, and raise them in strong and stable families. It is a time-honored recipe for producing bright (and happy) children.

Green Runway Lights

When I'm flying into Los Angeles International Airport at night, I sometimes look ahead to see the green runway lights that tell the captain where to land the plane. Captains know that if they bring their craft down between those boundaries, all should be well. In a similar way, parents need some runway lights—some guiding principles—that will help them raise their children. Without a beacon or two to direct their flight, they're blindly approaching a very complex and important task.

There are two fundamental principles that might be thought of as beacons to guide the parenting assignment. The first is to assure our kids that they are loved unconditionally. Without that awareness, little people wither like plants without water. The second is less understood but equally important. It requires us to teach our kids to respect parental authority. The child's acceptance of benevolent leadership, beginning at home, sets the stage for his attitude toward other forms of authority later in life. These two components, love and authority, are basic to the developmental needs of children.

By heeding these guiding lights on the runway, your child has a good chance of making a successful flight and a safe landing beyond the turbulence of adolescence.

PARENTING TEENS

Kids Are like Kites

The task of letting our children go can be a tough one for parents. It was described by the late Erma Bombeck as being rather like flying a kite in this manner: Mom and Dad run down the road hoping to catch a breeze. Eventually, and with much effort, they manage to hoist the kite a few feet in the air. Just when they think it is safely under way, great danger looms. It dives toward electrical lines and twirls perilously near the trees. It is a scary moment. Then, unexpectedly, a gust of wind catches the kite and carries it upward. Mom and Dad begin feeding line as rapidly as they can.

The kite then becomes difficult to hold. Parents reach the end of their line and begin to wonder what to do next. The little craft demands more freedom. It rises higher and higher. Dad stands on tiptoe to accommodate the tug. It is now grasped tenuously between his index finger and thumb, held upward toward the sky. Then comes the moment of release. The string slips through Dad's fingers, and the kite soars majestically into God's beautiful sky.

The kite is now a mere pinpoint of color in the sky. The parents are proud of what they've done—but sad to realize that their job is finished. It was a labor of love. But where did the years go?[1]

Parenting is an exhilarating and terrifying experience and one that was ordained from the beginning. But with the ultimate release, the parents' task is finished. The kite is free, and so, for the first time in twenty years, are they.

Choosing Your Battles with Care

One of the most delicate aspects of raising a teenager is figuring out what's worth a showdown and what isn't.

I remember talking to a waitress, a single mother, in a restaurant a few years ago. When she found out I was a psychologist, she began telling me about her twelve-year-old daughter.

"We've fought tooth and nail this whole year," she said. "It's been awful! We go at it every night—usually over the same issue."

"What do you argue about?" I asked.

The mother spelled it out. "Well, she's still a little girl, but she wants to shave her legs. I feel she's too young, but she gets so angry she won't even talk to me. What do you think I should do?"

"Lady," I said, "go buy your daughter a razor."

That twelve-year-old girl would soon be paddling into a time of life that would rock her canoe good and hard. Her mom, as a single mother, would be trying desperately to keep this rebellious teenager from getting into drugs, alcohol, and premarital sex. Truly, there would be many ravenous alligators in her river within a year or two. In that setting it seemed unwise to make a big deal over what was essentially a nonissue.

I've seen other parents fight enormous battles over what were really inconsequential matters. It is a great mistake. I urge you not to damage your relationship with your kids over behavior that has no great moral or social significance. There'll be plenty of real issues that will require you to stand like a rock. Save your big guns for those crucial confrontations, and pretend not to notice that which is trivial.

Compensatory Skills

It's not easy getting through adolescence today, and the effective parent must learn early how to brace his or her kids before those turbulent years arrive.

Perhaps the most painful aspect of growing up is related to the assault on self-esteem that is almost universal in today's teen society. Young people typically feel like fools and failures before they've even had a chance to get started in life. So how can parents prepare their younger children for the teenage years to come? Is there any way to make that passage to adulthood any easier and safer?

Well, one important approach is to teach boys and girls valuable skills with which to provide a centerpiece in their self-identity in years to come. They can benefit from learning about basketball, tennis, electronics, art, music, or even raising rabbits for fun and profit. It's not so much what you teach your child. The key is that he or she learn something with which to compensate when the whole world seems to be saying, "Who are you, and what is your significance as a human being?"

The teenager who has no answer to those questions is left unprotected at a very vulnerable time of life. Developing and honing skills with which to compensate may be one of the most valuable contributions parents can make during the elementary school years. It may even be worth requiring your carefree kid to take lessons, practice, compete, and learn something he or she will not fully appreciate for a few more years.

The Attack of the Killer Hormones

What is the process by which a happy, cooperative, twelve-year-old boy or girl suddenly turns into a sullen, depressed thirteen-year-old? It happens in almost every family.

There are two powerful forces that account for some of the adolescent behavior that drives parents crazy. The first is linked to the peer pressures that are common at that time. Much has been written about those influences. But there is a second, and I think more important, source of disruption of those years. It is related to the hormonal changes that not only transform the physical body, which we can see, but also revolutionize how kids think. For some (but not all) adolescents, human chemistry is in a state of imbalance for a few years, causing agitation, violent outbursts, depression, and flightiness. This upheaval can motivate a boy or girl to do things that make absolutely no sense to the adults who are watching anxiously on the sidelines. The hormonal firestorm operates much like premenstrual tension or menopause in women, destabilizing the self-concept and creating a sense of foreboding.

Parents often despair during the irrationality of this period. Everything they've tried to teach their sons and daughters seems to have misfired for a couple of years. Self-discipline, cleanliness, respect for authority, and common courtesy may give way to risk taking and all-around goofiness.

If that's where your child is today, I have good news for you. Better days are coming. That wacko kid will soon become a tower of strength and good judgment—if he doesn't do something destructive before his hormones settle down once more.

Teens Before Their Time

I s your mailbox stuffed with catalogs full of trendy designer clothes for every member of the family? Ours is. The other day I saw a pair of high-tech padded running shoes that cost nearly fifty dollars, and they were designed for toddlers who are barely able to walk.

More and more, we see adolescent clothes, attitudes, and values being marketed to younger and younger children. Those perfectly beautiful fashion dolls and the dating culture they inspire are aimed primarily at the elementary school-age market. Teenage stars, too, are promoted to the pre-teen set, which responds with appropriate crushes and fan mail. And rock and rap music, with adolescent and adult themes, is finding eager listeners among the very young.

This adolescent obsession can place our children on a very unnatural timetable, likely to reach the peak of sexual interest several years before it's due. That has obvious implications for their social and emotional health. I believe it is desirable to postpone the adolescent experience until it is summoned by the happy hormones. Therefore, I strongly recommend that parents screen the influences to which their children are exposed, keeping activities appropriate for each age.

While we can't isolate our kids from the world as it is, we don't have to turn our babies into teenyboppers.

Who's at Fault When Kids Go Bad?

Whose fault is it when a teenager gets into trouble? Who gets the blame when he or she skips school or sprays graffiti on a bridge or begins to experiment with drugs? Whom do we accuse?

In the eyes of culture, parents are inevitably responsible for the misbehavior of their teenagers, and certainly, many deserve that criticism. Some are alcoholics or child abusers, or they have otherwise damaged their kids through their own blunders. But it's time we admitted that the sons and daughters of some very loving, caring parents can go wrong, too.

Only in this century have we blamed all misbehavior of teenagers on their parents. In years past, if a kid went bad, he was a bad kid. Now it's inevitably the fault of his dear old mom and dad, who must have bungled his childhood in some way. Well, maybe, and maybe not. Adolescents are old enough to make irresponsible choices of their own, and some do stupid things despite the love and care they receive at home.

I would not seek to exonerate parents who have shortchanged their kids and treated them badly. But someone should speak on behalf of those good-as-gold moms and dads who did the best they could for their rebellious children. They deserve a pat on the back, not a slap in the face.

Getting Past the Negative Ions

Sometimes raising teenagers can be like sending an astronaut into space. Early space probes launched from Cape Canaveral in the 1960s created anxiety for the safety of the astronaut. It was especially intense when the spacecraft was reentering the earth's atmosphere. At the most dangerous part of the journey, negative ions would accumulate around the heat shield and interfere with radio contact for about seven minutes. Finally, the reassuring voice of Chris Kraft would break in and say, "We've made contact with Colonel Glenn again. Everything is A-OK."

In a very real sense, adolescence can be like that spacecraft. After the training of childhood, a thirteen-year-old is blasted into space with a flurry. Something like "negative ions" begins to interfere with communication just as the adults want to be assured of the child's safety. Why won't he talk to them? Why has he or she disappeared behind a wall of silence? It is a terrifying time.

Fortunately, in a few years, the first scratchy signals will begin to come through again, and contact will be reestablished. The negative environment will gradually dissipate and the "splashdown" during the early twenties can be a wonderful reunion for both generations.

Pachyderms and Teenagers

I once watched a documentary showing how Indian elephants are trained to serve their human masters, and I was struck by the parallel between these beautiful creatures and our fragile teenagers.

The training process for elephants begins shortly after capture with three days of total isolation. These pachyderms are remarkably social animals, and they react to their loneliness in the same way humans do. They grieve and fret and long for their peers. At the peak of their vulnerability, the elephants are brought to a nighttime ceremony of fire, where they are screamed at and intimidated for hours. By morning, half-crazed, the elephants have yielded; their wills have been broken. Forever after, they will be slaves to a new master.

We humans also have a great need for love and acceptance, especially during our adolescent years. And like elephants during the night of fire, teenagers are often subjected by their culture to a period of intense isolation and loneliness, which often leaves them feeling rejected, ridiculed, and ignored. Some quickly begin to lose their sense of independence. They become slaves to conformity and peer pressure.

Somehow we must teach our children, long before they are teenagers, that they need not follow the whims of adolescent society. They can lead, or they can follow. It's better to lead.

The Launch

There is a period in every young adult's life between ages sixteen and twenty-six that can literally shape or break his or her future. I call it the "Critical Decade." A person is transformed during those ten years from a kid who's still living at home and eating at the parents' table to a full-fledged adult who should be earning a living and taking complete charge of his or her life. Most of the decisions that will shape the next fifty years will be made during this era, including the choice of an occupation, the decision to marry or not to marry, and the establishment of values and principles by which life will be governed.

Some young adults move easily through the critical decade, but others have greater difficulty making decisions and getting on with life. They can't settle on a line of work, set reachable goals, channel their interests, or decide what to do next. So they sit around their parents' home and watch daytime television. Young people such as these remind me of a rocket on a launchpad. They are ready to blast through the stratosphere, but the engines just won't fire. For some, an explosion occurs that leaves debris all over the place.

There are ways to help sons and daughters get moving if they will accept the parents' help. Arrange visits to vocational counselors who can give interest inventories and occupational tests that can clarify goals. Take them on career visits, and introduce them to people working successfully in different professions.

The countdown is coming. Your young adult will either blast off or blow up. You might help make the difference.

Predators in the Tall Grass

A few years ago my family and I visited the magnificent wild-animal preserve known as the Serengeti in Tanzania. It had rained all day, and we eventually came to a stretch of road that was almost impassable. We were faced with a choice between two muddy paths but had no idea which to take. If we went the wrong way and became stuck, we would have spent the night there without food, water, or bathroom facilities. At that point our seventeen-year-old son, Ryan, volunteered to help.

"I'll run ahead and look at the two roads," he said. "Then I'll wave to let you know which is best."

The missionary who was with us said, "Um, Ryan, I don't think that is a very good idea. You just don't know what might be out there in the tall grass."

Eventually we chose what looked like the better of the two paths. But when we reached the place where the two trails came together, a huge male lion was crouched in the grass off to one side. He rolled his big yellow eyes and dared us to take him on. Ryan looked at that lion and agreed that it might be best to stay in the car!

In a manner of speaking, our experience on the Serengeti illustrates the passage from late adolescence to young adulthood. The journey goes smoothly and safely for some individuals. But a surprisingly large number of teens encounter unexpected "mud holes" that trap and hold them at an immature stage of development. Still others are plagued by dangerous predators. Among these are an addiction to alcohol or drugs, marriage to the wrong person, failure to achieve a coveted dream, suicide, homicide, or other criminal offenses.

It is, alas, very easy to make a very big mistake when young. Given the predators lurking in the tall grass, it does behoove us parents to stay very close to our sons and daughters on their road to adulthood.

You Don't Trust Me

If there's a magic bullet that teenagers use to manipulate their folks, it's these four words: You don't trust me!

The instant a young person accuses us of being suspicious and imagining the worst, we start backpedaling. "No, dear, it's not that I don't trust you being out with your friends or taking the car, it's just that I…" and then we run out of words. We're on the defensive, and the discussion is over.

Well, maybe it's time we recognized that trust is divisible. In other words, we can trust our children at some things but not at others. It's not an all-or-nothing proposition. This is the way the world of business works from day to day. Many of us are authorized, for example, to spend our company's money from certain accounts but not the whole corporate checkbook. I don't trust myself to attempt certain things like skydiving or bungee jumping, for another example.

So let's stop being suckered by our kids and boldly state that trust comes in stages. Some of it now and more later on.

Parents have the task of risking only what we can reasonably expect to be handled safely. To do more is not really trust; it's foolhardiness.

Talking to a Teen

There are some teenagers who sail right through the adolescent experience with hardly any evidence of turbulence. They make wonderful grades in school; they're a delight to their teachers and a treasure to their parents. But there are others, as we all know, who seem to declare war on the world and stay mad for the next ten years.

Mark Twain was referring to this second kind of kid when he wrote, "When a child turns 12, you should put him in a barrel, nail a lid down and feed him through a knot hole. When he turns 16, you should seal up the knot hole."[2] There are times when parents have reason to feel that way, to be sure.

Erma Bombeck said she wasn't going to pay two thousand dollars to straighten the teeth of a kid who never smiled. Another mother talked about how her son had been a chatterbox throughout childhood, but when he became a teenager, his vocabulary consisted of only nine word-phrases. They were "I dunno," "Maybe," "I forget," "Huh?" "No!" "Nope," "Yeah," "Who—me?" and "He did it."

What are you going to do if your sweet, cuddly, cooperative preteenager turns into a sullen, silent adolescent? The answer is, you go right on loving him or her. What is going on inside that youngster, hormonally and emotionally, explains much of what you see on the outside. But it won't always be that way. Better days are coming. The smile and a rich vocabulary will return. I promise.

The Hallway of Doors

I magine, if you will, a long dark hallway with a series of doors on either side. Written on each door is the name of an addiction, such as alcohol, tobacco, marijuana, hard drugs, gambling, pornography, and the like. Now, teenagers must walk down the hallway on this journey from childhood to adulthood. The temptation is very great to open one or more of the doors along the way. They can hear the beat of the music and the raucous laughter of their friends echoing from inside. The pressure to join them can be enormous. And it is very difficult to convince a fun-loving adolescent that he or she should stay in the dark hallway, which seems so boring and embarrassing.

Unfortunately, for a certain percentage of individuals who open one or more of these dangerous doors, a tragedy begins to unfold. If a person is susceptible—and there's no way to know in advance—he or she only has to crack the door an inch or two and a monster will run out and grab that young man or woman. Some will be held in its grip for the rest of their lives.

If you talk to an alcoholic about his or her addiction, you'll learn that it probably began casually—with no hint that life was about to take a radical and tragic turn. It all started with the opening of a door—probably during the teen years.

Sheep Led to Slaughter

I once saw a dramatic documentary film that featured a packinghouse where sheep were slaughtered. Huddled in pens were hundreds of nervous animals that seemed to sense danger in their unfamiliar surroundings. Then a gate was opened leading to a ramp and through a door to the right. In order to get the sheep to walk up that ramp, the workers used what is known as a "Judas goat." This is a goat that has been trained to lead the sheep into the slaughterhouse.

The goat confidently walked to the bottom of the ramp and looked back. Then he took a few more steps and stopped again. The sheep looked at each other skittishly and began moving toward the ramp. Eventually, they followed the confident goat to the top, where he went through another gate that closed behind him. This forced the sheep directly into the slaughterhouse. It was a dramatic illustration of herd behavior with deadly consequences.

There is a striking similarity between the sheep following the Judas goat and teenagers who succumb to peer pressure. Those who are more confident and rebellious often lead the timid into trouble. Some inject themselves with heroin or get involved with cocaine; others engage in dangerous sexual practices, drive while drinking, and engage in violent behavior. But why do they do such destructive things? Don't they care about their own lives and the future they are risking? Most of them do. But the pressure to conform—to follow the Judas goat—is even stronger than the need for security and well-being.

Adults have a similar problem. The prophet Isaiah observed it when he wrote, "We all, like sheep, have gone astray."[3]

PRIORITIES

The Disease of Materialism

I remember seeing an advertisement from a large bank that encouraged people to borrow money, asking the question: "What do you need to make you happy?" How foolish, I thought, to believe that a new car or a boat or even a house can hold the keys to personal satisfaction.

Materialism is a disease that infects the human family—and it's not a problem only in affluent cultures. Author and financial counselor Ron Blue tells the story of visiting a small, rural village in Africa. Ron asked a native there what was the biggest problem facing his village. The man said, "Materialism."

Ron was taken aback. He expected it to be the lack of food or medical attention, or perhaps problems with neighboring villages. But materialism? These villagers didn't have televisions or cars or satellite dishes—the sorts of things we associate with "the good life." But this villager told Ron, "If a man has a mud hut, he wants one made out of cow manure. If he has a cow manure hut, he wants a stone hut. If he has a thatch roof, he wants a tin roof. If he has one acre, he wants two. Materialism is a disease of the heart. It has nothing to do with where you live."

That's probably the simplest and best explanation of materialism I've heard. And it might hit pretty close to where you live.

Take a good hard look at the loved ones in your life—and then tell me where your real priorities are.

It's the Simple Things That Count

You don't have to spend huge amounts of money to have a meaningful family life. Children love the most simple, repetitive kinds of activities. They want to be read the same stories hundreds of times and hear the same jokes long after they've heard the punch lines. These interactions with parents are often more fun than expensive toys or special events.

A friend of mine once asked his grown children what they remembered most fondly from their childhood. Was it the vacations they took together or the trips to Disney World or the zoo? No, they told him. It was when he would get on the floor and wrestle with the four of them. They would gang-tackle the "old man" and laugh until their sides hurt. That's the way children think. The most meaningful activities within families are often those that focus on that which is spontaneous and personal.

This is why you can't buy your way out of parenting responsibilities, though many have tried. Busy and exhausted mothers and fathers, especially those who are affluent, sometimes attempt to pay off their deprived kids with toys, cars, and expensive experiences. It rarely works. What boys and girls want most is time spent with their parents—building things in the garage or singing in the car or hiking to an old fishing pond. No toy, to be played with alone, can ever compete with the enjoyment of such moments. And those moments will be remembered for a lifetime.

Heaven's Gate

You might remember the tragic account of the Heaven's Gate cult, whose thirty-nine members committed suicide in 1997. Their expectation of boarding a spaceship left the American people shocked and puzzled. What would cause so many seemingly healthy people to kill themselves in pursuit of a fantasy from outer space?

The cult might have been motivated unconsciously by the quest for significance and purpose that resides within the human spirit. To satisfy that search for meaning, each of us must answer numerous questions posed by life, including "Who am I?" "Why do I exist?" "Who created me?" and "Is there life after death?" People who are unable to find satisfactory answers to these questions become sitting ducks for the con men of our time. They often chase after crazy notions cooked up by gurus and self-appointed saviors, who tell lies to those who *need* to believe.

Someone explained it this way: "Superstition is the worm that exudes from the grave of a dead faith." In other words, when a person recognizes no god who can give meaning to life, there is a great void inside that aches to be filled. Frequently that individual will turn to hocus-pocus, magic, UFOs, and ancient myths to satisfy his or her deep longings. It would appear that the Heaven's Gate cult succumbed to that false teaching.

There is a lesson worth noting here for parents. We simply must give our children something in which to believe—not just something, but the only true source of Truth in the person of Jesus Christ. The failure to accomplish that quest for meaning can leave them vulnerable to bizarre cults. In regard to the Heaven's Gate cult, it sent thirty-nine people to their deaths while trying to flag down a passing spaceship.

The Greatest Danger

I'm often asked what I perceive to be the greatest threat to families today. I could talk, in response, about alcoholism, drug abuse, infidelity, and the other common causes of divorce. But there is another curse that accounts for more family breakups than the others combined. It is the simple matter of overcommitment and the tyranny of the urgent.

Husbands and wives who fill their lives with never-ending volumes of work are too exhausted to take walks together, to share their deeper feelings, to understand and meet each other's needs. They're even too worn out to have a meaningful sexual relationship, because fatigue is a destroyer of desire.

This breathless pace predominates in millions of households, leaving every member of the family frazzled and irritable. Husbands are moonlighting to bring home more money. Wives are on their own busy career track. Children are often ignored, and life goes speeding by in a deadly routine. Even some grandparents are too busy to keep the grandkids. I see this kind of overcommitment as the quickest route to the destruction of the family. And there simply must be a better way.

Some friends of mine recently sold their house and moved into a smaller and less expensive place just so they could lower their payments and reduce the hours required in the workplace. That kind of downward mobility is almost unheard of today—it's almost un-American. But when we reach the end of our lives and we look back on the things that mattered most, those precious relationships with people we love will rank at the top of the list.

If friends and family will be a treasure to us then, why not live like we believe it today? That may be the best advice I have ever given anyone— and the most difficult to implement.

Echo from Eternity

Vince Foster served as deputy counsel to U.S. president Bill Clinton until the night of July 20, 1993, when he allegedly committed suicide in a Washington DC park.[1] Controversy has swirled around the circumstances of his death to this day.

Regardless of where you come down on that issue, I want to share something related to it that I think you'll find interesting. Just eight weeks before his death, Foster was asked to speak to students graduating from the University of Arkansas School of Law. This is what he told the students on that occasion:

> A word about family. You have amply demonstrated that you are achievers willing to work hard, long hours and set aside your personal lives. But it reminds me of that observation that no one was ever heard to say on a deathbed: I wish I had spent more time at the office. Balance wisely your professional life and your family life. If you are fortunate to have children, your parents will warn you that your children will grow up and be gone before you know it. I can testify that it is true. God only allows us so many opportunities with our children to read a story, go fishing, play catch, and say our prayers together. Try not to miss a one of them.[2]

Vince Foster's words now echo back to us from eternity. To paraphrase his message: While you're climbing the ladder of success, don't forget your own family.

Dad, I Never Really Knew You

Several months ago I talked to a man who described one of the most painful experiences of his life. When he was seventeen years old, he was one of the stars on his high school football team. But his father, a very successful man in the city, was always too busy to come see him play.

Quickly the final game of the season came around, which happened to have been the state championship. The boy was desperate to have his dad there. The night of the big game, he was on the field warming up when he looked into the stadium just in time to see his father arrive with two other men, each wearing a business suit. They stood talking together for a moment or two and then left.

The man who told me this story is now fifty-eight years of age, and yet he had tears streaming down his cheeks as he relived that moment so long ago. It's been forty years since that night, and yet the rejection and pain are as vivid as ever. I was struck again by the awesome influence a father has in the lives of his children. When he is uninvolved, when he doesn't love or care for them, it creates a vacuum that reverberates for decades.

My friend's father died not long ago, and as he stood by his dad's body in the mortuary, he said, "Dad, I never really knew you. We could have shared so much love together—but you never had time for me."

"The Game of Life"

When my daughter, Danae, was a teenager, she came home one day and said, "Hey, Dad! There's a great new game out. I think you'll like it. It's called Monopoly." I just smiled.

We gathered the family together and set up the board. It didn't take the kids long to figure out that old Dad had played this game before. I soon owned all the best properties, including Boardwalk and Park Place. I even had Baltic and Mediterranean. My kids were squirming, and I was loving every minute of it.

About midnight I foreclosed on the last property and did a little victory dance. My family wasn't impressed. They went to bed and made me put the game away. As I began putting all of my money back in the box, a very empty feeling came over me. Everything that I had accumulated was gone. The excitement over riches was just an illusion. And then it occurred to me, *Hey, this isn't just the game of Monopoly that has caught my attention; this is the game of life. You sweat and strain to get ahead, but then one day, after a little chest pain or a wrong change of lanes on the freeway, the game ends. It all goes back in the box.* You leave this world just as naked as the day you came into it.

I once saw a bumper sticker that proclaimed, "He who dies with the most toys wins." That's wrong. It should say, "He who dies with the most toys dies anyway."

Fame

Society's fascination with Hollywood and celebrities has gone a little crazy. Millions idolize those who have achieved fame and fortune, but stardom does not provide the satisfaction that it advertises. Marilyn Monroe could have told us that.

Consider the adoration and respect accorded to Muhammad Ali in his prime. He was known around the world as "the prizefighter who couldn't be beaten." His picture appeared on the cover of *Sports Illustrated* more times than any athlete in history. Wherever he went, the cameras followed. Today, though, it's a different story.

Sportswriter Gary Smith spent some time with the ailing fighter at his home and asked to see his trophy room. Ali escorted him to a dark, damp barn beside his house. There, leaning against one wall was a board displaying mementos, photos from the "Thrilla in Manila," pictures of Ali dancing and punching and hoisting championship belts over his head. But the pictures were smeared with white streaks. Pigeons had made their home in the rafters. Ali picked up the board and turned it around, face to the wall. Then, as he started to leave, Smith heard him mumble, "I had the world, and it wasn't nothin'. Look now."[3]

Fame is fleeting, even for those few who achieve it. If that is where you are searching for meaning, you are not likely to find it.

Bill and Frank

One of the most powerful stories in the history of the Olympic Games involved a canoeing specialist named Bill Havens. He was a shoo-in, I'm told, to win a gold medal in the 1924 Olympic Games in Paris.

But a few months before the Games were held, he learned that his wife would likely give birth to their first child while he was away. She told him that she could make it on her own, but this was a milestone Bill just didn't want to miss. So he surprised everyone and stayed home. Bill greeted his infant son, Frank, into the world on August 1, 1924. Though he always wondered what might have been, he said he never regretted his decision.

Well, he poured his life into that little lad and shared with him a love for the rapids. Twenty-four years passed, and the Olympic Games were held in Helsinki, Finland. This time Frank Havens was chosen to compete in the canoeing event. The day after the competition, Bill received a telegram from his son that read: "Dear Dad, Thanks for waiting around for me to be born in 1924. I'm coming home with the gold medal that you should have won." It was signed, "Your loving son, Frank."[4]

Many would question Bill Havens's decision to miss his big opportunity in Paris, but he never wavered. He wanted his family to know that they always came first, no matter what. And that made him a hero to a little boy named Frank.

SELF-ESTEEM
AND SELF-RESPECT

Happily Ever After

Have you ever stopped to consider just how effectively children's traditional literature teaches kids, and especially little girls, that they must be beautiful—or else? Many of the age-old stories center around physical attractiveness in one form or another.

Take, for example, The Ugly Duckling. This is a story about an unhappy little bird who was rejected by the better-looking ducks. Fortunately for him, he had a beautiful swan inside that surfaced in young adulthood. The story does not mention the ugly duckling who grew up to be an ugly duck!

Then there's Sleeping Beauty. Why wasn't she called Sleeping Ugly? Because the prince wouldn't have awakened her with a gentle kiss! He would have let a homely little princess go on resting.

How about Rudolph the Red-Nosed Reindeer? Rudolph had a weird nose that caused his little reindeer friends to laugh and call him names. They wouldn't let poor Rudolph join in the reindeer games. This story has nothing to do with reindeer. It has everything to do with children. This is how they treat the physically peculiar.

Don't forget Snow White, who was resented by the evil queen. That's why she asked the question, "Mirror, mirror on the wall, who's the fairest of them all?" The queen was green with envy over Snow White's stunning beauty.

And how about Dumbo the elephant? Dumbo was ridiculed for having big floppy ears until he used them to fly.

Then there is the all-time favorite: Cinderella. It wasn't the carriage and the horses that shook up the prince when she arrived at the ball. You can bet Cinderella was a pretty little thing.

These age-old stories are fun to read, and many generations of children have loved them. But we should understand their hidden messages, even if we continue to share them. There's a very serious side to the emphasis on beauty in the literature of the young. Little girls, especially, can begin to believe that those who are unattractive are unworthy as human beings. That is a very destructive idea.

Mutual Admiration

Our sense of self-respect is often based on the reactions, positive or negative, of those around us. That is especially true in the intimate context of marriage.

Dr. Paul Brand was a flight surgeon during World War II. He tells in one of his books of a fine young man named Peter Foster, who was a Royal Air Force pilot. Foster flew a Hurricane, which was a fighter with a design flaw: The single-propeller engine was mounted in the front, and the fuel lines ran past the cockpit. In a direct hit, the pilot would instantly be engulfed in flames before he could eject. The consequences were often tragic.

Some RAF pilots caught in that inferno would undergo ten or twenty surgeries to reconstruct their faces. Peter Foster was one of those downed pilots whose face was burned beyond recognition. But Foster had the support of his family and the love of his fiancée. She assured him that nothing had changed except a few millimeters of skin. Two years later they were married.

Foster said of his wife, "She became my mirror. She gave me a new image of myself. When I look at her, she gives me a warm, loving smile that tells me I'm OK."

That's the way marriage ought to work, even when disfigurement has not occurred. It should be a mutual-admiration society that builds the self-esteem of both partners and overlooks a million flaws that could otherwise be destructive. There's a word for that kind of commitment: We call it *love*.

Shifting Standards of Human Worth

Millions of adults today suffer from low self-esteem. Most of them learned to hate their bodies or their circumstances when they were in adolescence and continued at war with themselves into the adult years. It is self-imposed ridicule, and there are few experiences in life that are more destructive.

If you're among the vast number of people who have never come to terms with their own identity, let me offer a word of advice that may be helpful. The standards by which you have assessed yourself are themselves changing and fickle.

Maxwell Maltz, the plastic surgeon who wrote *Psycho-Cybernetics*, said women came to him in the 1920s requesting that their breasts be reduced in size. More recently women wanted them augmented with silicone (until the health risks became understood).

False values!

In King Solomon's biblical love song, the bride asked her groom to overlook her dark skin, which occurred from exposure to the sun. But today she'd be the pride of the beach.

False values!

Modern women are ashamed to admit that they carry an extra ten pounds of weight, yet Rembrandt would have loved to paint their plump bodies.

False values!

The standards by which we measure ourselves are arbitrary, temporary, and unfair. It's a system designed to undermine confidence. Your personal worth is not really dependent on the opinions of others or the fluctuating values that they represent. Every person alive is entitled to dignity, self-respect, and confidence.

The sooner you can accept the transcending worth of your humanness as a gift from God, the sooner you can rid yourself of the burden of low self-esteem.

The Victimization of Everyone

Has it ever seemed like the whole world is stacked against you—and that you are never given a fair shake? Have you ever said, "Well, what did you expect? Nothing ever goes right for me anyway"?

This defeatist attitude could be expected among those who have been through severe illness, abuse, or disabilities. But something different has been happening in recent years. Large numbers of Americans have begun perceiving themselves as victims of some sort of unfairness—as though someone was out to get them. As more and more individuals perceive themselves in that way, their anger at one another intensifies.

Consider the classifications of some of the people who feel discriminated against. They include Hispanics, African-Americans, Asians, Jews, Native Americans, women, children, the elderly, the sick, the poor, the uneducated, and now even white males, who are not supposed to feel discriminated against. It's what I call the "victimization of everyone."

Now obviously, discrimination, racism, sexism, and ageism are still very serious problems in this culture, and we need to resolve them. I would not underestimate the impact of them. But it doesn't help for people to conclude that they're all being "had" in one way or another. That mindset is demoralizing. It paralyzes us emotionally, and it leads us to conclude, "What's the use? I can't win!"

Eleanor Roosevelt, who had some very serious handicaps in life, once said, "No one can make you feel inferior without your consent."[1] Well, it's true. And no one can attack your self-worth but you yourself.

A No-Knock Policy

One of the most common characteristics of a person who feels inadequate and inferior is that he talks about his deficiencies to anyone who will listen.

For example, an overweight person feels compelled to apologize to his companions for ordering a hot-fudge sundae. He echoes what he imagines they're already thinking. "I'm fat enough without eating this," he says, scooping up the cherry and the syrup with his spoon. Likewise, a woman who thinks she's unintelligent will admit freely, "I'm really bad at math. I can hardly add two plus two."

This kind of self-denigration is not as uncommon as one might think. Listen to yourself in the weeks to come. You might be surprised by how often you emphasize your faults to your friends. While you're babbling about all of your inadequacies, the listener is formulating his impressions of you. He will later see you and treat you according to the evidence that you've provided. After all, you're the expert on that subject.

This understanding is particularly important for children, who should be taught what I call a "no-knock policy" by their parents. Kids should learn that constant self-ridicule can simply become a bad habit.

There's a big difference between accepting blame when it's valid and simply chattering about one's inferiority. It really boils down to this: Self-respect breeds respect among others. Children are fully capable of understanding that fact.

Princess Diana

Diana, princess of Wales, was arguably one of the most glamorous and beautiful women in the world. Paparazzi hounded her for photographs right to the last moments of her life. During the latter years, Diana could generate more support for a particular cause or charity than any other celebrity.

Given this enormous influence—this glamour and beauty—isn't it interesting that the princess disliked what she saw in the mirror? She struggled with a poor body image that led to an eating disorder known as bulimia. How could a woman of such remarkable charm fall victim to self-loathing and depression?

Perhaps Diana's poor self-concept wasn't as strange as it might have seemed. Our value system, promoted so vigorously by Hollywood and the entertainment industry, is arranged so that very few women feel particularly good about their physical appearance. Even the Miss America or Miss Universe competitors will admit, if they're honest, that they are aware of their physical flaws. If those who are blessed with great beauty often deal with self-hatred, imagine how immature, gangly teenagers feel about the imperfect bodies with which they're born.

The beauty cult infects hundreds of millions of people with a sense of inadequacy and inferiority. Indeed, even Diana, princess of Wales, fell into its snare.

The Most Rejected Man of His Time

He began his life with all the classic handicaps and disadvantages. His mother was a dominating woman who found it difficult to love anyone. She gave him no affection, no training, and no discipline during his early years. When he was thirteen, a school psychologist commented that he probably didn't even know the meaning of the word *love*. During adolescence, the girls would have nothing to do with him and he fought with the boys.

After failing at every pursuit, including a stint in the U.S. Marine Corps, he fled the country. He married a Russian girl, but she also began to hold him in contempt. She could outfight him, and she learned to bully him. Finally, she forced him to leave.

After days of loneliness, he went home, fell on his knees, and literally begged her to take him back. He wept at her feet, but she laughed at him and made fun of his sexual impotency in front of a friend. Finally, he pleaded no more. No one wanted him. No one had ever wanted him. He was perhaps the most rejected man of his time.

The next day he was a strangely different man. He arose, went to the garage, and took down a rifle he had hidden there. He carried it with him to his newly acquired job at a book-storage building. And from a window on the sixth floor of that building, shortly after noon, November 22, 1963, he sent two shells crashing into the head of President John Fitzgerald Kennedy.

Lee Harvey Oswald—the rejected, unlovable failure—killed the man who, more than any other person on earth, embodied all the success, beauty, wealth, and family affection that Oswald lacked. In firing that rifle, he utilized the one skill he had learned in his entire, miserable lifetime.[2]

Barbie and Her Pals

M any years ago I wrote in one of my books that I didn't like what Barbie dolls did to little girls who played with them. Parents still ask why I feel that way.

Let me begin by admitting that my daughter played with Barbie dolls for years, despite my own views on this subject. I just didn't have the heart to take them away from her. Nevertheless, I *wished* Barbie would go away. There could be no better method for teaching the worship of beauty and materialism than is modeled by these dolls. If we intentionally sought to drill our little girls on the necessity of growing up rich and gorgeous, we could do no better than has already been done.

Did you ever see an ugly Barbie doll? Has she ever had even the slightest imperfection? No chance! She oozes femininity and sex appeal. Her hair is thick and gleaming—loaded with "body" (whatever that is). Her airbrushed skin is without flaw or blemish (except for a little statement on her bottom that says she was "Made in Hong Kong"). Such an idealized image creates later pressures when a real-life thirteen-year-old takes her first long look in the mirror. No doubt about it—Barbie she ain't!

In short, I'm philosophically opposed to these dolls primarily because they establish unrealistic expectations in years to come. That's my first concern. I'll share the second in my next commentary.

Teenie Barbies

I've discussed my concerns about Barbie dolls and their impact on little girls who become absorbed with them. They create an image of physical perfection that most girls will never be able to meet. I'm convinced that many self-image problems in the teen years are linked to a standard of beauty that is emphasized throughout childhood.

There is another concern that worries me. Barbie dolls (and their many competitors) usher girls into adolescent experiences long before they are ready for them. Instead of three- and four-year-old girls playing with stuffed animals, balls, cars, model horses, and the traditional memorabilia of childhood, they are learning to fantasize about life as a teenager. Barbie and her boyfriend, Ken, go on dates, learn to dance, drive expensive sports cars, get suntans, take camping trips, exchange marriage vows, and have babies (hopefully in that order). The entire adolescent culture, with its emphasis on sexual awareness, is illustrated to very young girls, who ought to be thinking about more childish things. This places them on an unnatural timetable likely to reach the peak of sexual interest several years before it is due—with all the obvious implications for their social and emotional health.

Regardless of what you do with Barbie and her gorgeous buddies, I strongly recommend that you postpone the adolescent experience until your children get there. They will have plenty of time afterward to be bona fide teenagers.

No More Showers

When I was a teenager, all the students were required to shower after gym class at school. The coach would look us over to make sure we were clean before sending us on our way. Students who didn't shower didn't receive a passable grade. But those days are just about over.

The heightening sensitivity of kids today makes them unwilling to disrobe in front of one another. They vary so much in maturity during the middle school years that some are grown and others are still little prepubescent kids. Thus, it is humiliating for the undeveloped youngster to put his or her body on display in front of the wolf pack.

I served as a school psychologist in earlier days and dealt with this problem. I remember a high school sophomore who absolutely refused to shower because of the ridicule he was getting. After seeing what was happening, I agreed that he shouldn't be forced to humiliate himself in front of his friends five days a week. I successfully pled his case to the coach.

That lad's reaction was unusual twenty years ago. Today it is common. The body consciousness of our culture has sensitized many children and teenagers to their imperfections. Thus, school showers are being phased out. Another reason is that coaches and teachers have become leery of false charges of sexual abuse.[3]

The outcome? Teachers have to work in classrooms populated by adolescents who smell like gymnasiums—or worse. It's a sign of the times.

SEX, DATING, AND PURITY

New Rules to the Courtship Game

There was a time when young girls were taught to be reserved—to keep a tight rein on their impulses—especially when it came to matters of the heart. They would never have asked a boy for a date, or even have made the first telephone call. But much of that has changed, I believe, for the worse.

The sexual revolution of the past thirty years has had a dramatic effect on the way the courtship game is played. Boys have traditionally been the initiators, and girls were once quite content to be the responders. But what we're seeing now is a new sexual aggressiveness among females that has many parents worried.

Some girls are so bold sexually and have such a hard-charging approach that males are intimidated and anxious to escape that firepower. The male ego is constructed in such a way that many men are uncomfortable if not in pursuit. Even in this day when the old restrictions and taboos for women have fallen away, I believe it's still appropriate for parents to teach their girls a certain reserve, a certain self-respect when it comes to romantic relationships. This is especially true during the awkward experiences of early adolescence.

It may be difficult for a girl to pull in her horns a bit, but she'll be more successful and less vulnerable by attracting the object of her affection, rather than trying to run him down.

The Great Condom Caper

Young people are being told today that they can have sex with numerous partners if they will simply protect themselves by using condoms. It sounds simple, doesn't it? What does medical science tell us about the effectiveness of these devices?

A careful investigation revealed that condoms failed to prevent pregnancy among married couples 15.7 percent of the time.[1] Another study showed that they failed 36 percent of the time in preventing pregnancy among young unmarried minority women.[2] This dismal record explains why there's a word for people who rely on condoms as a means of birth control. We call them *parents*.

Now remember that a woman can conceive only two or three days per month, whereas HIV and other sexually transmitted diseases (STDs) can be transmitted 365 days per year. If condoms are not used properly, if they are defective, or if they slip just once, the results can be disastrous. One mistake after hundreds of protected episodes is all it takes to catch an STD. The young victim who's told by his or her elders that this little latex device makes intercourse safe may not know what lies ahead. Lifelong pain and even death are being risked for a brief moment of pleasure. What a burden to place on an immature mind and body!

The only way to protect yourself from deadly diseases is to practice abstinence as long as you are single, then marry an uninfected person (if you marry at all), and live together in mutual fidelity for life. That is the biblical plan—and it is the only behavior that makes sense during an epidemic of STDs.

Children Having Children

What should parents do when a teenage daughter comes to them and speaks those electrifying words, "Mom and Dad, I'm pregnant"?

Responding to a teen pregnancy is one of the most difficult trials parents are ever asked to face. When the news breaks, it's reasonable to feel anger toward the girl who has brought this problem into their lives. How dare this kid do something so stupid and hurtful to herself and the entire family!

Once Mom and Dad have caught their breath, however, a more rational and loving response is appropriate. This is no time for recriminations. Their daughter needs understanding and guidance now more than ever, and they are the ones to provide it. She'll face many important decisions in the next few months, and she'll need a calm, rational, and caring mother and father to assist in determining the best path to take.

If parents can call up that kind of strength, they and their daughter will eventually enjoy the bond that often develops between people who have survived a crisis together.

The Great Safe-Sex Scam

For more than two decades, the federal government has spent nearly three billion dollars to promote safe-sex ideology among American teenagers. It's time we asked what taxpayers have gotten for their money and what sex-education programs have achieved by such a massive effort.

In the 1970s, there were two sexually transmitted diseases (STDs) at epidemic proportions in this country, syphilis and gonorrhea. Both were entirely curable by brief antibiotic therapy. Today, more than twenty STDs infect large percentages of the population. Some of them, notably gonorrhea, are becoming resistant to most antibiotics and may soon be beyond the reach of medical science.

Of even greater concern are numerous sexually transmitted viruses, which now infect more than fifty million people. They include herpes, human papillomavirus (HVP), HIV, and AIDS-related illnesses. There is *no* cure for any of these diseases. Those who have them, which includes one in five Americans, will suffer for the rest of their lives! Many will ultimately succumb to their ravages.

There has been a conspiracy of silence about the dangers of these diseases. How many young women know, for example, that four thousand deaths per year are attributed to HPV?[3] Yet it is a known fact that condoms do not protect against this virus. It is transmitted from genital areas not protected by condoms. A yearlong study of female students visiting the medical center at the University of California, Berkeley, showed that 47 percent of them were infected![4]

This is the legacy of an insane policy. Young people are suffering because the truth has been withheld from them. Those who depend on condoms to protect them during promiscuous sex usually wind up sick, pregnant, or both.

Without question, the safe-sex program is a disaster in the making!

Children at Risk

From 1985 to 1986 I served on the U.S. Attorney General's Commission on Pornography, which turned out to be one of the most difficult assignments of my life. For eighteen months I had the unenviable responsibility, with ten other commissioners, of examining the most wretched material ever published. Many people think obscenity consists of airbrushed nudity as seen in popular men's magazines. In reality, much of it involves graphic violence against women, depictions of bestiality, the killing of children, and other subjects that I can't describe in this setting. Our commission ultimately made twenty-six recommendations for changes in the law, each of which was passed by Congress and signed by the president. [5]

I regret to say, unfortunately, that the progress we made in the fight against obscenity has been lost. There are no limits now because of the Internet. Everything we witnessed during that investigation can be accessed by any twelve-year-old child with a computer and a modem. He or she can log on to websites that are clearly illegal. Material can be printed on high-resolution copiers that equals anything found in adult stores.

Not only can these images be found on the Internet—they can't be avoided. Kids are lured with attractive bait designed to snare the innocent. For example, clicking on "toys" can introduce them to sex toys; clicking on "love horses" can produce images of bestiality; clicking on "little girls" can introduce child pornography or those who prey on kids.

As a child psychologist, I want to emphasize that obscenity is *terribly* destructive to boys and girls. It is especially dangerous to boys in the early adolescent years. It can lead to lifelong addictions and teach them to associate sex with violence.

Despite these dangers, our United States Supreme Court has ruled that the law designed to protect children from this curse is unconstitutional. [6] What a shame!

Let me plead with parents to monitor what your kids are doing on that innocent-looking computer. To put a desktop or a laptop in a child's bedroom is tantamount to inviting a stranger into your home and giving him or her access to your most precious possession!

Bundy's Last Words

In 1989 I conducted a videotaped interview with Ted Bundy just a few hours before he was to be executed for killing at least twenty-eight women and girls. During that candid conversation in the shadow of the electric chair, Bundy described how he had come to be addicted to pornography since finding detective magazines in a dump when he was thirteen years of age. He was later obsessed by violent images that led to the murders of many women and a twelve-year-old girl. After spending twelve years on death row and meeting many killers, Bundy became convinced that pornography has a horrible effect on men, who are particularly susceptible to it. He argued passionately, there in the last hours of his life, for additional limits on the sale and distribution of obscene materials.

This is a portion of Bundy's last words:

> I can only hope that those who I have harmed and those who I have caused so much grief—even if they don't believe my expression of sorrow and remorse—will believe what I'm saying now, that there is loose in their towns, in their communities, people like me today whose dangerous impulses are being fueled day in and day out by violence in the media in its various forms, particularly sexualized violence.... And what scares and appalls me, Dr. Dobson, is...when I see what's on cable TV, some of the movies, some of the violence in the movies that come into homes today [is] stuff that they wouldn't [have shown] in X-rated adult theaters thirty years ago.... But I'll tell you, there are lots of other kids playing in streets around this country today who are going to be dead tomorrow and the next day and the next day and next month, because other young people are reading the kinds of things and seeing the kinds of things that are available in the media today.[7]

I am certain that Bundy was right. Every few days we read about another boy or girl who has been sexually assaulted and brutally murdered. When a suspect is identified, authorities typically find boxes of pornography in his possession, much of it depicting violence against women and children. It has become a very familiar pattern.

Waiting for the Glue to Dry

Dr. Desmond Morris, well-known researcher and author, spent many years studying the institution of marriage and the factors that contribute to long-term intimacy. A relationship that fails to survive, he said, can usually be traced to the dating days when the bond between a man and woman was inadequately cemented. And what interfered with the bond? It is likely to result from physical intimacy occurring too early in the relationship. Instead of taking the time to know each other—to talk and laugh and share lovers' secrets—the couple engages in early sexual activity. Such familiarity interferes with intimacy and weakens the marital bond ever after.[8]

It may be a stretch, but this understanding reminds me of my efforts to build model airplanes as a kid. My friends made wonderful planes out of balsa wood, but I could never get one finished. Why? Because I was too impatient to wait for the glue to dry. I just couldn't keep my hands off the pieces long enough for them to congeal.

Romantic relationships that begin with touching, kissing, fondling, and intercourse in the early dating days do damage to the bond. So if you want to enjoy an intimate friendship that will remain vibrant for a lifetime, the key is simple: Just keep your hands off one another until the glue dries.

SIBLINGS

Raising Cain and Abel, Too

If mothers were asked to indicate the most irritating feature of child rearing, I'm convinced that sibling rivalry would get their overwhelming vote. Little children, and older ones, too, are not content just to hate each other in private. They attack one another like miniature warriors, arguing, fighting, hitting, screaming, and probing for weaknesses in the defensive line. It's enough to drive Mom and Dad up the wall.

But it doesn't have to be that way. It is neither necessary nor healthy to allow children to attack each other and make life miserable for the adults around them. You may not harmonize the kids' relationship entirely, but at least you can avoid making it worse. I recommend that parents be careful not to inflame the natural jealousies between children. Ever since time began, brothers and sisters have resented each other's successes and competed for parental attention. That's why mothers and fathers should be very careful to avoid casual comments that favor one of their kids over the others, especially in the areas of physical attractiveness, intelligence, and athletic ability.

Those are the three raw nerves on which self-esteem hangs in Western societies. To refer to a child as "my pretty daughter" or to a son as "the smart one" is to set off raging emotions in those who perceive themselves to be ugly or dumb. Sensitivity in those areas will reduce the antagonism between siblings and create a more harmonious tone for every member of the family.

Fences Make Good Neighbors

Sibling rivalry was responsible for the first murder on record when Cain killed Abel, and it's been occurring at a furious pace ever since.

While conflict between brothers and sisters occurs in virtually every family, it is possible to lessen the antagonism and create a more family-friendly atmosphere in the home. The key is for parents to enforce a reasonable set of boundaries between warring factions.

Robert Frost said, "Good fences make good neighbors." I agree. People get along better when there are reasonable boundaries between them and when law and order are evident. Suppose I lived in a frontier town where there were no police officers, no courts, and no city ordinances. My neighbor and I would be much more likely to fuss with one another than in a modern society where the laws are known and a mechanism exists for their enforcement.

And so it is with children in a family. Everyone gets along better when there are reasonable rules that are enforced with fairness. Otherwise, chaos reigns. When the older child can make life miserable for a younger boy or girl or when the younger can break the toys and mess up the things of his big brother or sister, hatred is more likely to be fomented. It is a consequence of the lawless environment in which they live.

That's why I strongly recommend that parents set up reasonable rules for harmonious living at home and then enforce them with the full weight of their authority. Only then can children live peacefully with their little rivals down the hall.

29

SINGLE PARENTING

With Love to the Single Mom

Imagine the agony a single parent goes through when required by court order to put his or her children on an airplane, all alone, for an extended visitation with the other parent.

One single mom described her feelings. She said:

> I stand in the terminal, and I watch the kids' airplane disappear into the clouds. I feel an incredible sense of loss. The loneliness immediately starts to set in. I worry constantly about their safety, but I resist the urge to call every hour to see how they're doing. And when they do call me to tell me how much fun they're having, I grieve over the fact that they're having a life completely separate from my own. My only consolation is knowing that they're coming home soon. But I'm haunted by the fear that they won't want to come home with me.

For the single parent who identifies with this hurting mother, there may be a way to get through the painful days of waiting. Instead of seeing this time alone as a period of isolation and deprivation, view it as an opportunity to recharge the batteries and reinvigorate the spirit. Spend some uninterrupted time with friends. Read an inspirational book, or return to a hobby that you've set aside. Fill your day with things that are impossible amid the responsibility of child care, recognizing that your children will benefit from your rehabilitation. They'll return to a reenergized parent, instead of one coming off weeks of depression.

Raising Boys Alone

One of the greatest contributions a single mother can make for a young son is to find him a mentor.

In her book *Mothers and Sons,* the late Jean Lush talked about the challenges single mothers face in raising sons. The ages four to six are especially important and difficult. A boy at that age still loves his mother, but he feels the need to separate from her and gravitate toward a masculine image. If he has a father in the home, he'll usually want to spend more time with his dad apart from his mother and sisters.

But what advice can be given to a mother who is raising a son alone? First, she must understand that he has needs that she is not best equipped to meet. Her best option is to recruit a man who can act as a mentor to her son—one who can serve as a masculine role model. Of course, good mentors can be difficult to find. Single mothers should consider friends, relatives, or neighbors who can offer as little as an hour or two a month. In a pinch, a mature high schooler who likes kids could even be "rented" to play ball or go fishing with a boy in need.

Single women who belong to a Christian church should be able to find support for their boys among the male members of the community. Scripture commands people of faith to care for children without fathers. Isaiah 1:17 states, "Take up the cause of the fatherless; plead the case of the widow." Jesus Himself took boys and girls on His lap and said, "Whoever welcomes one such child in my name welcomes me" (Matthew 18:5). I believe it is our responsibility as Christian men to help single mothers with their difficult parenting tasks.

Certainly, single mothers have many demands on their time and energy, but the effort to find a mentor for their sons might be the most worthwhile contribution they can make.

Robin in a Rainstorm

A single mother sent a story to me recently that helped explain the loneliness and stress faced by those who are raising their children alone. She said she was looking out her window one drizzly day, and she saw an unfolding drama. A mother robin and her brood of chicks were perched in the nest of a scrub-oak tree. As the rain poured down, the mother bird covered her chirping little chicks beneath her extended wings. Then the hail began to fall. Instead of tucking her head safely in the nest, the mother robin raised her head upward and took the blows to protect her young. All of the chicks made it safely through the storm.

What a graphic illustration of the perils of single parenting! That responsibility of raising kids alone is unrelenting, requiring moms and dads to earn a living, cook, clean, supervise homework, take care of sick kids, and so on. Beyond these day-by-day duties, they must figure out how to meet their own personal and spiritual needs. Taken in context, this may be one of the toughest assignments on earth. Single parents, whether mothers or fathers, need our continued support and prayers.

To those who are taking the blows on behalf of their children, let me assure you that a better day is coming. The storm won't last forever. A beautiful rainbow will soon appear. And when the job has been completed and a brood of healthy little birds has been raised, there will be sweet benefits for the parents who don't fly away.

30

STRESS

The Toughest Hour of the Day

Why is the evening drive time in a big city called "the rush hour" when nothing moves? The real rush hour occurs when people arrive at home.

Early evening is a time when everyone is hungry and tempers are short. Two-career parents usually come home irritable and tired. But their children are unsympathetic and need immediate attention. It is a setup for conflict.

There are some things you can do to help defuse this rush-hour time bomb. First, you might want to telephone your children before you leave work in the afternoon. This can give you a head start in dealing with any troubles that might be brewing at home. Second, make a conscious effort during the commute to disengage from the responsibilities of the job. Listen to some "elevator music," and unwind from the cares of the day.

Concerning the dinner meal, it is wise to do as much as possible in the morning or the night before. Crock-Pot–type dinners that have cooked all day or those that can go straight from the refrigerator to the oven will relieve pressure at a time when stress is the greatest. The quicker everyone can eat and raise their blood sugar, the better. Then spend some time with the kids before homework and baths begin. You might take the dog on a neighborhood walk or play catch in the backyard. Finally, get the kids in bed and reserve a few moments of tranquillity for yourselves.

OK, let's admit it. There's no easy way to get through "rush hour" five nights a week, but with a little forethought, it can be less stressful.

No Place to Hide

Have you ever fantasized about running away from all the pressures and stresses of today's high-tech world? Surely there is a place somewhere on the globe where the pace is slower and the living is easy. Why don't we just pack up and transplant ourselves there—lock, stock, and family dog?

That dream motivated a family in 1940 to move to an island called Guadalcanal in the Coral Sea. But two years later war broke out in the Pacific, and the couple found themselves witnessing a battle in their front yard. Obviously, they had chosen the wrong place.

Where can today's families go to escape the noise and hubbub of city life? How about a small island in the Caribbean south of Cuba, called Grand Cayman? Vacationers to this resort say it is the closest thing to paradise on earth. The six thousand residents pay no taxes.[1] The water around them is calm and warm, and there are orchids growing everywhere. Sounds good, doesn't it? But there's a catch. Recent medical studies revealed that the two major ailments suffered by the citizens of Grand Cayman are "hypertension" and "anxiety neuroses." Life on a tropical beach is not what it appears.

Could it be that the stresses and pressures with which we struggle actually come from within? They will plague us no matter where we live until we learn to deal with circumstances as they are. We might as well stay and bloom where we're planted, because there's simply no place to hide.

Stress and the Human Body

I wonder if you've ever had an experience like the one I went through a few years ago. I had gone to bed early one night and was lying there waiting for my wife to finish some work in the kitchen. As she had loaded the dishwasher, I could near its gentle *swoosh-swooshing* from the other end of the house. Then, suddenly, I realized that it wasn't the machine I was hearing at all. It was the squishy, rhythmic sound of my own heart—beating in my ear instead of in my chest where it belonged. This pounding went on for a week and began to drive me crazy.

I finally made an appointment with a specialist who told me that the muscles in my face were squeezing the vessels near my ear. I was actually hearing the blood trying to get past those constricted channels.

"It's not dangerous," I was told by the doctor.

"What would cause it?" I asked.

"It's stress," he told me. "You're running too fast."

I said, "I suppose you're going to tell me to slow down."

"Nope," he replied with a smile. "I can't control my own life. Why would I try to tell you how to manage yours?"

The doctor had it right. Stress is a fact of life in this high-speed culture. It can make your head hurt, your intestines retch, and your blood pressure soar. It can even make your ears pound and squish in the night. Stress is the price we pay for being racehorses instead of cows.

But why do we live such hectic lives? What could possibly motivate us to run the human engine at full throttle until it threatens to blow up or melt down? I don't know, but I'm convinced that this kind of breathless living is an assault on common sense and good judgment. It not only threatens our physical bodies but is also the ultimate destroyer of meaningful family life.

31

SUPPORT AND SECURITY

Through the Darkness

I'm told that when I was a very small child—maybe two years of age— my family lived in a one-bedroom apartment, and my little bed was located beside the bed of my parents. My father said that it was common during that time for him to awaken at night to a little voice that was whispering, "Daddy? Daddy? Daddy?"

My father would answer quietly, "What, Jimmy?"

And I would say, "Hold my hand!"

My dad would reach across the darkness and grope for my little hand, finally engulfing it in his. He said later that the instant he had my hand firmly in his grip, my arm would become limp and my breathing deep and regular. I would immediately fall back to sleep.

You see, I only wanted to know that he was there! Until the day he died, I continued to reach for him—for his assurance, for his guidance—but mostly just to know that he was there.

Then, so very quickly, I found myself in my dad's place. And I wanted to be there for my children—not just a name on their birth certificate, but a strong, warm, and loving presence in their lives.

You see, a dad occupies a place in a child's heart that no one else can satisfy. So to all the men out there who are blessed to be called fathers, I urge you to be there for the little ones in your life who call you "Dad."

Defending the Underdog

Every school has dozens of boys and girls who are at the bottom of the social hierarchy. Some are physically unattractive, some are slow learners, and some are simply unable to make friends and find a comfortable place in the school environment.

The key question is, what should teachers do when they see one of these disrespected children being ridiculed and taunted by his peers? Some would say, "Kids will be kids. Stay out of the conflict, and let the children work out their differences for themselves." I disagree emphatically.

When a strong, loving teacher comes to the aid of the least respected child in the class, something dramatic occurs in the emotional climate of the room. Every child seems to utter an audible sigh of relief. The same thought bounces around in many little heads: *If that kid is safe from ridicule, then I must be safe, too.* By defending the least popular child in the classroom, the teacher is demonstrating that she respects everyone and that she will fight for anyone who is being treated unfairly.

One of the values children cherish most is justice. They are, conversely, very uneasy in a world of injustice and abuse. Therefore, when we teach children kindness and respect for others by insisting on civility in our classrooms, we're laying a foundation for human kindness in the world of adulthood to come.

I say again to teachers: Defend the most defenseless child in your classroom.

My Kid's a Superstar

How do you feel about those bumper stickers that say, "My Child Is an Honor Student at Washington Junior High School"? I imagine they are irritating to parents whose kids are less gifted. One such mother put this sticker on her car: "My Kid Can Beat Up Your Honor Student."

We all feel good about the successes of our children, and well we should. Problems arise, however, when the pride of the family is riding on the shoulders of an immature child. Boys and girls should know that they're accepted simply because of their own unique worth.

I'm reminded of John McKay, the former great football coach at the University of Southern California. I saw him interviewed on television some years ago when his son John Jr. was a successful football player on the USC team. The interviewer asked Coach McKay to comment on the pride he must have felt over his son's accomplishments. His answer was most impressive.

"Yes," he said, "I'm pleased that John has had a good season this year. He does a fine job, and I'm proud of him. But I would be just as proud if he had never played the game at all."

Coach McKay was saying, in effect, that John's football talent is recognized and appreciated, but his human worth does not depend on his ability to play football. Thus, his son would not lose his respect if the next season brought failure and disappointment. John's place in his dad's heart was secure, independent of his performance.

I wish every child could say the same.

Necessary Separation

We've written about divorce and its lifelong consequences for children. But what about parent–child separation that occurs for reasons other than divorce? Is the pain any less intense for kids when the disruptive factors are unrelated to family disintegration?

Research confirms that the consequences of *any* parent–child separation are severe. In one study of fathers whose jobs required them to be away from their families for long periods of time, the children tended to experience numerous negative reactions, including anger, rejection, depression, low self-esteem, and commonly, a decline in school performance. Those findings have been confirmed in other contexts as well.

I have reason to understand the pain brought by family separation, because I experienced it when I was six years old. My mother and father left me with my aunt for six months while they traveled. I sat on my mother's lap while she told me how much she loved me and that she and my father would come back for me as soon as they could. Then they drove away as the sun dropped below the horizon. I sat on the floor in the dark for an unknown period of time, fighting back the tears that engulfed me. That sorrowful evening was so intense that its pain can be recalled instantly today, more than five decades later.

In short, even when parent–child separation occurs for valid reasons in a loving home, a boy or girl frequently interprets parental departure as evidence of rejection. Nothing short of necessity should cause us to put children through that experience.

I Wish

A sixth-grade teacher shared with me the results of a creative-writing project assigned to her class. She asked the kids to complete a series of sentences that began with the phrase "I wish…" The teacher expected her students to write about bicycles, toys, animals, and trips to theme parks. She was wrong. Instead, twenty of the thirty students made references to the breakup of their families or conflict at home. These are some of their actual comments:

"I wish my parents wouldn't fight, and I wish my father would come back."

"I wish I would get straight A's so my dad would love me."

"I wish my mother didn't have a boyfriend."

"I wish I had one mom and one dad so the kids wouldn't make fun of me. I have three moms and three dads, and they botch up my life."

"I wish I had an M-1 rifle so I could shoot those who make fun of me."

I know it's hardly front-page news that the family is in trouble today, but it continues to distress me to see little children like these struggling at a time when simply growing up is a major undertaking. Millions of their peers are caught in the same snare. Every aspect of their young lives is influenced by family instability during their developmental years. Without gaining access to professional counseling somewhere along the way, many of these kids will drag their problems into future relationships. Then the pattern of disintegration will repeat itself in the next generation.

Returning to the responses given by the sixth-grade students, I wonder how your *own* children would complete a sentence that began with the words "I wish…" You might want to ask them sometime.

Little Ears

Parents need to be very careful about comments made within hearing of their children. Youngsters are often very capable of understanding and remembering insulting remarks. When I was five years old, for example, I came running into a room just in time to hear my father say something unkind to several other men. I still recall that remark made many years ago. My dad didn't intend to hurt me through his insensitivity to others, and he later apologized. But his carelessness became part of the permanent record in my mind.

I've heard similar mistakes made by parents seeking my advice after a speaking engagement. They would begin talking openly with me about a problem one of their kids was having. As they described an embarrassing characteristic, I would notice that the kids were standing by their moms and listening intently. They may never forget insulting comments made in their hearing.

Surprisingly, it's not just insensitive parents who make such blunders. I once referred to a neurologist a bright, nine-year-old boy who was having a severe learning problem. After giving the lad a thorough examination, the neurologist invited the parents and their son into the office for a consultation. Then he diagnosed the "brain damage" in front of the wide-eyed little patient as though he couldn't hear those awesome words or comprehend their implications. I'm certain the child never forgot them.

Sensitivity is the key. It means tuning in to the thoughts and feelings of our kids during their vulnerable years.

Why They Kill

A major effort has been made in the past few years to learn why so many teenagers growing up in the inner city are often shockingly violent. What we're seeing now is different from criminal behavior of the past.

Today young people are committing horrible and senseless acts of brutality without remorse—such as the two boys, ages twelve and thirteen, who beat a man to death outside a convenience store just for the pleasure of watching him die. Another boy shot a man sitting in a car at a stop sign. When asked why he did it, the boy said, "Because he looked at me."[1]

After extensive research, scientists have concluded that violent behavior is often related to early child abuse and neglect. When babies spend three days or more in dirty diapers or when they are burned, beaten, or ignored, their blood is flooded with stress hormones—cortisol and adrenaline among others. These hormones bombard and damage the brains of those children. So for the rest of their lives, they will not think and feel what others do. They actually lose the capacity to empathize with those who suffer.[2]

The unmistakable conclusion is that babies and young children are incredibly vulnerable between birth and three years of age. If their families don't protect and care for them, society will pay a terrible price for it in the years to come.

TRIALS

Perseverance

Abraham Lincoln was perhaps the greatest of all U.S. presidents. He led the nation through its darkest hour, preserved the union, and issued the historic Emancipation Proclamation. What is equally impressive, however, is the way he handled adversity.

You may have heard about his many disappointments and failures, but perhaps your children haven't. Let me cite the record again in memory of this great man. In 1831 he suffered a business failure. In 1832 he was defeated in a bid for the state legislature. In 1833 he underwent a second business failure. In 1835 his fiancée died. In 1836 he experienced a mental breakdown. In 1838 he was defeated for speaker of the state legislature. In 1840 he was defeated for the office of elector. In 1843 he was defeated for land officer. In 1846 he won an election for the Congress. But in 1848 he was defeated in his reelection bid. In 1855 he was defeated in a run for the Senate. In 1856 he was defeated in his bid for vice president. In 1858 he lost again in another attempt at the Senate, and in 1860 he was elected president of the United States.[1]

What incredible perseverance in the face of adversity! It is a lesson in history that every schoolchild should be taught to appreciate.

A Forgotten Monument

Last summer I was in a picturesque little town called Garmisch in southern Germany, and I happened to notice a small monument erected in memory of the young men who died in the First World War.

It caught my attention because, as an American, I've always thought of our war dead as heroes and the enemy losses as, well, the enemy. But there on a bronze plaque were the names of boys who had actually lived in that beautiful village and who suffered, bled, and died for their country. About twenty men were listed, along with their ranks and dates of death, from 1914 to 1918. I stood reading those names and wondering what stories they concealed and what their losses meant to the loved ones waiting in that little town.

Then I walked to the other side of the monument and saw another bronze plaque listing the dead from the Second World War, 1939 to 1945. Something immediately jumped out at me. Many of the last names were the same. It was obvious that the young men who had lost their lives in that Great War had left little boys behind who grew up in time to die in the next. It also meant there were women in Garmisch who lost their husbands in World War I only to have their sons die two decades later on other battlefields.

This little journey into history emphasized for me once more that it is families that suffer most from the ravages of war.

Lowering Expectations

Astrophysicist Stephen Hawking may be the most intelligent man on earth, being compared by some to Albert Einstein. But Hawking has a rare degenerative neuromuscular disorder called amyotrophic lateral sclerosis (ALS syndrome). It has left him virtually paralyzed. He manipulates a computer with the tips of his fingers and thereby communicates his calculations and thoughts.

Dr. Hawking has offered a very insightful perspective on his disorder. He said that before becoming ill he was bored by what he called "a pointless existence." He drank too much and did very little work. But after learning that he may have had only a few years to live, life suddenly took on new meaning. He was actually happier than before.

Hawking explained the paradox this way: "When one's expectations are reduced to zero, one really appreciates everything that one does have."[3]

It's true. Everything becomes meaningful to those who are dying: a sunrise, a walk in the park, the laughter of children. But those who believe life owes them a free ride are often miserable. The high incidence of depression in Western nations, and maybe even the tragic rate of divorce, are linked in part to unrealistic expectations.

May I suggest that we accept our circumstances as they are and not demand more than life can deliver?

Going Down for the Third Time

When my wife, Shirley, and I were first married, we took a weekend trip to a local resort. She quickly put on her swimsuit and jumped into the pool before I could get there. She was surrounded by sunbathers and muscular lifeguards, who sat basking in the sun.

Shirley is not a strong swimmer and began to tire as she reached the deep end of the pool. The more she flailed at the water, the more exhausted she became. She began to be seized by panic.

I'm going to drown! she thought. *There's no way I can make it.*

All Shirley had to do was scream for help and the lifeguards and sixteen male swimmers would have been at her side. But to do so would have embarrassed her in front of all those gorgeous sunbathers. She decided to risk drowning rather than humiliate herself. Fortunately, she managed to splash her way to the edge, clinging there coughing, sputtering, and gasping for air.

That story reminds me of the people who are going under but are still unwilling to call for help. Some are alcoholics who deny they have a problem. Some are teenage druggies who can't admit they are hooked. Some even commit suicide rather than reach for the help that is readily available.

If you're drowning in a deep pool, call for help. Don't let your pride take you to the bottom.

Little Boy Blue

There's a classic poem by Eugene Field called "Little Boy Blue" that my father used to quote to me when I was a child, and it made me cry. It had great meaning for me then, even as a youngster, but the words took on new significance when I became a father. Let me share it with you today.

The little toy dog is covered with dust,
But sturdy and staunch he stands;
And the little toy soldier is red with rust,
And the musket moulds in his hands.
Time was when the little toy dog was new,
And the soldier was passing fair;
And that was the time when our Little Boy Blue
Kissed them and put them there.

"Now, don't you go till I come," he said,
"And don't you make any noise!"
So, toddling off to his trundle-bed,
He dreamt of the pretty toys;
And, as he was dreaming, an angel song
Awakened our Little Boy Blue.
Oh! the years are many, the years are long,
But the little toy friends are true!

Aye, faithful to Little Boy Blue they stand,
Each in the same old place
Awaiting the touch of a little hand
The smile of a little face;
And they wonder, as waiting the long years through
In the dust of that little chair,
What has become of our Little Boy Blue,
Since he kissed them and put them there.[3]

This poem is dedicated to those mothers and fathers who have lost a child in recent years. My prayers are with you.

Bees and Flies

I heard recently about an experiment in which twelve bees were placed in a jar in a darkened room. A light was beamed onto the bottom of the glass, and then the lid was removed. Instinctively, the bees flew toward the light and couldn't escape. All of the bees died trying to buzz their way through the bottom of the jar.

Next the researchers took twelve common houseflies and repeated the experiment. Within seconds the flies had found their way out of the jar. It is known that bees are more intelligent than flies, and their survival instincts are usually better defined. Yet it was those very instincts that doomed the bees.[4]

I wonder how often our own preconceived notions get in the way of common sense. My father, for example, hated automatic transmissions on automobiles because he learned to drive with stick shifts. I've fallen into similar patterns. Until 1992 I wrote books with pencils on yellow pads. I did that for years after word processors were available. The twentieth century was almost over before I decided to join it.

Rigidity and the force of habit can also cause us to do things that make no sense. What illogical ideas are you holding onto these days? It's a question worth pondering.

Ride down the Rogue

Many years ago my family and I took a raft trip down the Rogue River in Oregon. It almost became my last ride. After floating serenely for two days, I was suddenly thrown into the turbulent river. It seemed like an eternity before I came to the surface, only to discover I couldn't breathe. A bandanna that had been wrapped around my neck was now plastered across my mouth and held there by my glasses, which were strapped to my head. Just as I clawed free and gasped for air, churning water hit me in the face and gurgled into my lungs. I definitely considered the possibility that I was drowning. Fortunately, I managed to pull myself back into the raft, where I lay sucking air for about twenty minutes.

I've thought often about that experience in the ensuing years and concluded that life often resembles that beautiful Rogue River. There are long stretches when the water is calm and serene. You can see your reflection as you lean out of the raft. The scenery is gorgeous, and the river carries you peacefully downstream. Then without warning you are thrown overboard and taken to the bottom. Suddenly, you're gasping for air and thinking you're going to drown for sure.

It would be helpful for young people to know that this *will* happen to them sooner or later. No one travels down the river of life without encountering the rapids. There will be moments of serenity and beauty. But there will also be times of sheer terror when they'll be at the mercy of the good Lord.

It's all part of the ride.

Chippie the Parakeet

Author Max Lucado reported a delightful story about a parakeet named Chippie, who had a very bad day. It began when the bird's owner decided to clean his cage with a vacuum cleaner. She was almost finished when the phone rang, so she turned around to answer it. Before she knew it, Chippie was gone. In a panic, she unsnapped the top of the vacuum and ripped open the bag. There was Chippie, covered in dirt and gasping for air. She carried him to the bathroom and rinsed him off under the faucet. Then realizing that Chippie was cold and wet, she reached for the hair dryer. Chippie never knew what hit him

His owner was asked a few days later how he was recovering.

"Well," she replied, "Chippie doesn't sing much anymore. He just sits and stares."[5]

Have you ever felt like that? One minute you're whistling through life, and the next you're caught up in a whirlwind of stress. You're running frantically through the airport and arrive at the gate just in time to see your plane take off. The table is set for guests when you see smoke curling out of the kitchen. These annoyances of life strike when we least expect them, and they always leave us dazed and disoriented.

The next time life sucks you into its vortex, hang on and make the best of it. But unlike the experience of Chippie, don't ever let the song go out of your life.

Men of the Civil War

One of the most fascinating aspects of the U.S. Civil War is the toughness and determination of both Yankee and Rebel soldiers. Their lives were filled with deprivation and danger that is hardly imaginable today. It was common for the troops to march for weeks and then plunge directly into combat without rest. The fighting would continue for days, interspersed with sleepless nights on the ground—sometimes in a freezing rain or snow. The staple was a dry biscuit called hardtack, which shredded their intestinal tracts and left them undernourished.

Men stood rifle to rifle and slaughtered one another like flies. After one particularly bloody battle in 1862, five thousand bodies lay in an area of about two square miles. Many of the wounded remained where they fell for twelve or fourteen hours, with their groans and cries echoing through the countryside.[6]

I'm not glorifying the horrors of war certainly, but I am amazed that the troops didn't crack under these awful circumstances. They were committed to their cause, be they Yankees or Rebels, and nothing was going to deter them.

I do wonder in today's affluent times if our generation would make a similar sacrifice if required to defend our most cherished ideals. Would I? Would you?

UNDERSTANDING YOUR CHILD

Two Kinds of Kids

Have you noticed there are two kinds of kids in the world? Yes, there are boys and girls, but they differ in another important way, too. We can divide them into two categories according to their basic temperaments.

The first is composed of "compliant kids," those who sleep through the night from the second week of life. They coo at their grandparents, and they smile while their diapers are being changed. They never spit up on the way to the grocery store or the doctor's office because that would be inconvenient for their parents. During later childhood they love to keep their rooms clean and they do their homework brilliantly without being asked.

Then there are the children we might call "strong-willed kids." They get their mothers' attention long before birth because they start scratching their initials on the walls and kicking like crazy. They enter the world smoking a cigar, yelling about the temperature in the delivery room, and complaining about the utter incompetence of the nursing staff. From about eighteen months forward, they want to run things and tell everyone else what to do. Their favorite word is *no!*

Compliant children are a breeze to raise, of course, but the tougher kids can turn out fine, too. The trick is to shape that strong will during the early years without breaking the spirit. This is done by setting boundaries very clearly and then enforcing them with loving firmness. Even the toughest kids find security in a structured environment where other people's rights, as well as their own, are protected. That task is one of the most important challenges of parenthood.

When it is done right, even the most independent child can learn to be responsible and self-disciplined.

Protecting the Compliant Child

We've talked about children whose temperaments are naturally compliant, compared with those who are born with tough, assertive personalities. For some reason, every parent with two or more children is probably blessed with at least one of each.

When one child is a stick of dynamite and the other is an all-star sweetheart, the cooperative, gentle individual can easily be taken for granted. If there's an unpleasant job to be done, she may be expected to do it because Mom and Dad just don't have the energy to fight with the tiger. When it is necessary for one child to sacrifice or do without, there's a tendency to pick the one who won't complain as loudly. Under these circumstances, the compliant child comes out on the short end of the stick.

The consequences of such inequity should be obvious. The responsible child often becomes angry over time. She has a sense of powerlessness and resentment that simmers below the surface. He's like the older brother in the parable of the Prodigal Son told by Jesus. He didn't rebel against his father, but he resented the attention given to his irresponsible brother. That's a typical response. I strongly recommend that parents seek to balance the scales in dealing with the compliant child. Make sure he gets his fair share of parental attention. Help him find ways to cope with his overbearing sibling. And, within reason, give him the right to make his own decisions.

There's nothing simple about raising kids. Even the "easiest" of them need our very best effort.

Blank Slate or Complex Individual?

Does a newborn baby come into the world with a complex personality, or is that child a blank slate on which experience will write?

In years past, behavioral scientists believed newborns had no temperamental or emotional characteristics upon arrival from the womb. Their little personalities were formed entirely by the experiences that came their way in ensuing years. But most parents knew better. Every mother of two or more children was convinced that each of her infants had a different personality—a different feel—from the very first time he or she was held. Now, after years of research, numerous authorities in child development acknowledge that those mothers were right.

One important study identified nine characteristics that varied in babies—such as moodiness, level of activity, and responsiveness. They also found that the differences from child to child tended to persist into later life. It is my belief that babies differ in infinite ways that define our humanness and our individuality. And how foolish of us to have thought otherwise. If every snowflake that falls has its own design and if every grain of sand at the seashore is unique, it makes no sense to suppose that children are stamped out as though they were manufactured by Henry Ford.

I'm not denying the importance of the environment and human experience in shaping who we are and how we think, but there can be no doubt that each person on earth is truly a one-of-a-kind creation from the earliest moments of life. There are no assembly lines in God's scheme of things.

The Class Clown

I'll bet you remember him—the kid who could make everyone crack up at the most inopportune times. He was a trial to his teachers, an embarrassment to his parents, and an utter delight to every child who wanted to escape the boredom of school. And there are millions of them on the job today. It's my belief that boards of education assign at least one clown to every class to make sure that schoolteachers earn every dollar of their salaries.

These skilled little disrupters are usually boys. They often have reading or other academic problems. They may be small in stature, although not always, and they'll do anything for a laugh. Their parents and teachers may not recognize that behind the boisterous behavior is often the pain of inferiority.

You see, humor is a classic response to feelings of low self-esteem. That's why within many successful comedians is the memory of a hurting little boy or girl. Jonathan Winters's parents were divorced when he was seven years old, and he said he used to cry when he was alone because other children teased him about not having a father. Joan Rivers frequently jokes about her unattractiveness as a girl. She says she was such a dog her father had to throw a bone down the aisle to get her married. And so it goes.

These and other comedians got their training during childhood, using humor as a defense against childhood hurts. That's also the inspiration for the class clown. By making an enormous joke out of everything, he conceals the self-doubt that churns inside.

Understanding that should help us meet his needs and manage him more effectively.

Nature or Nurture?

For many decades behavioral scientists believed that newborns arrived into the world completely devoid of personality. The environment then stamped its unique characteristics on boys and girls during their developmental years. At one time most of the best-known psychologists in the world ascribed to this theory. Unfortunately, they were wrong.

We know now that heredity plays the larger role in the development of human temperament. This is the conclusion of meticulous research conducted over many years at the University of Minnesota. The researchers identified more than one hundred identical twins who had been separated near the time of birth. They were raised in varying cultures, religions, and locations, and for a variety of reasons. Because each set of twins shared the same genetic structure, it became possible for the researchers to examine the impact of inheritance by comparing their similarities and their differences on many variables. From these and other studies, it became clear that much of the personality, perhaps 70 percent or more, is inherited. Our genes influence such qualities as creativity, wisdom, loving-kindness, vigor, longevity, intelligence, and even the joy of living.[1]

Consider the brothers known as the "Jim twins," who were separated until they were thirty-nine years old. Their similarities were astonishing. Both married women named Linda, owned dogs named Toy, suffered from migraine headaches, chain-smoked, liked beer, drove Chevys, and served as sheriff's deputies. Their personalities and attitudes were virtual carbon copies.[2] This has become a very familiar pattern seen by researchers.

What do these findings mean? Are we mere puppets on a string, playing out a predetermined course without free will or personal choices? Not at all. Unlike birds and mammals that act according to instinct, humans are capable of rational thought and independent action. We don't act on every sexual urge, for example, despite our genetic underpinnings. Heredity provides a nudge in a particular direction—an impulse or inclination—but one that can be brought under the control of our rational processes.

Obviously, these findings are of enormous significance to our understanding of human behavior. They change everything, especially our understanding of children.

Go with the Flow

Some kids appear to be born to lead, and others seem to be made to follow. And that fact can be a cause of concern for parents at times.

One mother told me that her compliant, easygoing child was being picked on and beat up every day in nursery school. She urged him to defend himself, but it contradicted his very nature to even think about standing up to the bullies. Finally, his frustration became so great that he decided to heed his mother's advice. As they drove to school one day he said, "Mom, if those kids pick on me again today…I'm…I'm…I'm going to beat them up—slightly!"

How does a kid beat up someone slightly? I don't know, but it made perfect sense to this compliant lad.

Parents sometimes worry about this kind of easygoing, passive child—especially if the child is a boy. Followers in this society are sometimes less respected than aggressive leaders, and they can be seen as wimpy or spineless. And yet, the beauty of the human personality is seen in its marvelous complexity. There is a place for the wonderful variety of personalities that find expression in a child. After all, if two people are identical in temperament and point of view, it's obvious that one of them is unnecessary.

My advice to parents is to accept, appreciate, and cultivate the personality with which your little child is born. He need not fit a preconceived mold. That youngster is, thankfully, one of a kind.

Temperaments and Kids

Let's look at two kinds of children who are seen in every school classroom. Those in the first category are by nature rather organized boys and girls (more girls than boys) who care about details. They take the learning process very seriously and assume full responsibility for assignments given. To do poorly on a test would depress them for several days. Parents of these children don't have to monitor their progress to keep them working; it is their way of life, and it is consistent with their temperaments.

The second category of children includes the boys and girls (more boys than girls) who just don't fit in with the structure of the classroom. They're sloppy, disorganized, and flighty. They have a natural aversion to work, and they love to play. They can't wait for success, so they hurry on without it. Like bacteria that gradually become immune to antibiotics, the classic underachievers become impervious to adult pressure. They withstand a storm of parental protest every few weeks, and then when no one's looking, they slip back into apathy. They don't even hear the assignments being given in school, and they seem not to be embarrassed in the least when they fail to complete them. If they graduate at all, it's not gonna be cum laude; it'll be "Thank You, Laudy."

We really should talk more about these disorganized children because God sure made a lot of them. They drive their parents to distraction, and their unwillingness to work can turn their homes into World War III. I'll offer some suggestions that may be helpful in another commentary.

The Shy Child

I heard about a twelve-year-old boy who had never spoken a word in his life. His parents and his siblings thought he couldn't talk because they'd never heard his voice. Then one day the boy's mother placed a bowl of soup in front of him, and he took one spoonful. He pushed it away and said, "This is slop! I won't eat any more of it!"

The family was ecstatic. The boy had actually spoken a complete sentence! The father jumped up gleefully and said, "Why haven't you ever talked to us before?"

"Because," the boy said, "up until now, everything's been OK."

There are many shy kids among us who just don't do much talking. When they meet new people, they stand with their tongues in their cheeks and look down as though they're ashamed. Their parents wish they would be more assertive.

The question is, why are these kids so introverted and withdrawn? The answer is that they're born that way. According to the New York Longitudinal Study, shyness occurs in about 15 percent of children and tends to be a lifelong characteristic.[3] It is a function of heredity and temperament.

You can teach the social graces to a shy child, but it isn't wise to tamper with the basic personality. Instead, accept him or her exactly as designed. There's not another child on earth quite like that unique individual.

Fresh Graves

I've recently become aware of an outrageous and tragic situation occurring in Brazil and other Latin American countries. It concerns the plight of unwanted street children who are suffering unthinkable abuse.

It's been estimated that in Brazil alone, between 6 and 10 million kids live on the streets with no adult supervision. They have no families and no means of support, so they form lawless packs, begging and stealing for food during the day, then huddling together for warmth at night. Prostitution, crime, and disease are their way of life. Some of them actually live in sewers like rats. Roughly two-thirds of the young girls either commit suicide or are murdered before their eighteenth birthday.[4]

The police look on these children as vermin to be exterminated. Unbelievably, they shoot them to clean up the city. A recent news story revealed that approximately three children per day are hunted down and killed on the streets of Rio de Janeiro. A few years ago when the Earth Summit was held in that city, large numbers of homeless children were rounded up and murdered before the dignitaries arrived.[5] CNN televised row upon row of fresh little graves, where the children were buried.

I wonder sometimes if the world is any more civilized now than it was when the Nazis began gassing their victims. It's time for us to speak out against this brutality and to support humanitarian organizations that can help.

How can we do less?

Inexplicable Behavior

A very puzzled mother once asked me, "Why is it that some kids with every advantage and opportunity seem to turn out bad, while others raised in terrible homes become pillars of the community?" It's a good question.

I stood there nodding my head as this mother went on to tell stories of neglectful and couldn't-care-less parents who somehow raised model citizens. I could have cited a number of examples myself, because the fact is, environment simply doesn't account for everything. There's something else within us that makes us who we are. Some behavior is caused, and some plainly isn't. Remember that the same boiling water that softens the carrot also hardens the egg. Likewise, some youngsters react positively to certain circumstances while others react negatively. We don't know why.

What we do know is that children are more than the sum total of their experiences. They're more than the product of their nutrition or even their genetic inheritance. They are certainly more than their parents' influence. They are uniquely crafted individuals, every one of them, and they're capable of independent and rational thought that's not attributable to any source. That's what makes them human, and that's what also makes the task of parenting so challenging but also so rewarding. We don't need to take all the blame when they go wrong, but neither should we take the full credit when they excel.

NOTES

Chapter 1: Boundaries

1. "Yankelovich Monitor," Yankelovich Partners. http://www.yankelovich.com.
2. Ibid.

Chapter 2: Communication

1. Sybil Ferguson, *Woman's Day*, February 17, 1980.
2. Marilyn Elias, "Family Dinners Nourish Ties with Teenagers," *USA Today,* August 18, 1997.

Chapter 3: Community and Compassion

1. Charles Swindoll, *Come Before Winter* (Sisters, OR: Multnomah, 1985), p. 36.
2. John Donne, "Devotions upon Emergent Occasions," in John Bartlett, *Familiar Quotations,* ed. Justin Kaplan, 16th ed. (Boston: Little, Brown and Company, 1992), p. 231.

Chapter 4: Confidence Through Encouragement

1. Dick Korthals, "A Gentle Touch," *Focus on the Family*, 1992.

Chapter 7: Divorce

1. Cited in Barbara Vobejda, "Children of Divorce Heal Slowly, Study Finds; Scholar's Latest Evidence in Influential Series," *Washington Post,* June 3, 1997.
2. J.S. Wallerstein and J.B. Helley, "Effects of Divorce on the Visiting Father/Child Relationship," *American Journal of Psychiatry,* December 1980.

Chapter 8: Education and Learning

1. Home School Legal Defense Association. http://www.hslda.org.
2. James C. Dobson, *The New Dare to Discipline* (Wheaton, IL: Tyndale House, 1992), pp. 105-6.

Chapter 9: Emotions

1. *Cradles of Eminence* is out of print; however, the information can be found in Mildred G. Goertzel, *Three Hundred Eminent Personalities* (San Francisco: Jossey-Bass, 1978).

Chapter 10: Fatherhood

1. David Blankenhorn, "The Good Family Man: Fatherhood and the Pursuit of Happiness in America," An Institute for American Values working paper for the Symposium on Fatherhood in America, *Institutes for American Values,* November 2001.
2. Michael D. Lemonick, "Young, Single and Out of Control," *Time*, October 13, 1997.
3. "Births to Teens, Unmarried Women, and Prenatal Care: 1985–1994," *Statistical Abstract of the United States, 1997,* table no. 96, p. 78.
4. General Douglas MacArthur, "Duty, Honor, Country," given at West Point, May 12, 1962.

Chapter 11: Getting Older

1. L.M. Boyd, *Boyd's Book of Odd Facts* (New York: Signet, 1980), p. 50.
2. Anonymous.

Chapter 12: Grace and Forgiveness

1. *Focus on the Family*, December 20, 1982.
2. "A Community in Crisis," *Focus on the Family*, January 5, 1998.

Chapter 13: Health and Safety

1. *Family Circle*, February 26, 1985.
2. Peter Brimelow, "The Lost Children," *Forbes*, December 29, 1997.
3. *Fetal Alcohol Syndrome Factsheet*, Missouri Department of Mental Health, Division of Alcohol and Drug Abuse.
4. Judges 13.
5. Sandra Boodman, "Researchers Study Obesity in Children," *Washington Post*, June 13, 1995, p. 210.
6. Tim Friend, "Heart Disease Awaits Today's Soft-Living Kids," *USA Today*, November 15, 1994, p. 10.
7. *Family News in Focus*, March 6, 1992.
8. "Needle Park Closes," CNN, February 26, 1992.
9. Greg Harrington, "Ears to You: Protecting Your Hearing Now to Help Avoid Problems When You're Older," *Atlanta Journal and Constitution*, January 19, 1998.
10. Linda Roach Monroe, "An Exercise in Common Sense: You Don't Have to Knock Yourself Out at the Gym to Live Longer," *Los Angeles Times*, February 20, 1990.
11. Study done by Penn State University and reported in *Archives of Pediatric and Adolescent Medicine*, December 1997.

Chapter 15: Joy

1. Erma Bombeck, *The Family That Plays Together...(Gets on Each Other's Nerves)* (New York: Warner Communications, 1978).
2. Cited in Sam Venable, "Live a Dog's Life? We Lowly Humans Aren't That Lucky," *Knoxville News-Sentinel*, March 24, 1998.

Chapter 16: Legacy

1. *Mom Is Very Sick: Here's How to Help*, Focus on the Family. Out of print.
2. Jane Fullerton, "ER Doctor Joins Team for Reform," *Arkansas Democrat-Gazette*, May 28, 1994.
3. Dale Turner, "'Dagwood' Image Hides the True Value of Fatherhood—It's No Minor Task to Mold Young Lives," *Seattle Times*, June 19, 1993.
4. Karl Murray, "The 36th (Ulster) Division, and the Battle of the Somme, 1916," *The Great War*. http://36thulsterdivision.com/sommewww.htm.
5. Ibid.

Chapter 17: Life Lessons

1. James C. Dobson, *Straight Talk* (Dallas: Word, 1991), pp. 33-34.
2. "U.S. Naval Institute Proceedings," cited in Stephen Covey, *The Seven Habits of Highly Effective People* (New York: Simon & Schuster, 1989), p. 33.

3. Robert Fulghum, *It Was on Fire When I Lay Down on It* (New York: Villard Books, 1989), pp. 17-20.

Chapter 19: Marriage

1. Dr. Archibald Hart, Fuller Theological Seminary, Pasadena, California.
2. *World Book Encyclopedia,* 1996, s.v. "Taj Mahal."
3. Quoted by Max Lucado, *The Applause of Heaven* (Dallas: Word, 1990), p. 132.
4. Ibid.

Chapter 20: Money

1. Anne Stewart, "The American Way," *Associated Press*, November 23, 1997.
2. Denise Duclax, "Questions about the 'Inheritance Boom,'" *American Bankers Association Journal*, December 1996, p. 47.
3. John Sedgwick, *Rich Kids: America's Young Heirs and Heiresses: How They Love and Hate Their Money* (New York: William Morrow & Company, 1985).
4. Donna Partow, *Homemade Business* (Colorado Springs, CO: Focus on the Family, 1991).
5. National Debt Clock, maintained by the Concord Coalition.

Chapter 22: Parenting

1. Per Ola D'Aulaire and Emily D'Aulaire, "Now What Are They Doing at That Crazy St. John the Divine?" *Smithsonian*, December 1992, p. 32.
2. Elisabeth Elliot, *Discipline: The Glad Surrender* (Ada, MI: Fleming H. Revell, 1985).

Chapter 23: Parenting Children

1. Janet McConnaughey, "Study of Romanian Orphans Shows Importance of Touch," *Associated Press,* October 28, 1997.
2. P.W. Juscyzk and E.A. Hohne, "Infants' Memory for Spoken Words," *Science,* September 26, 1997, p. 1984ff.
3. Rachel Ellis, "Parents Beware: Little Ears Are Listening," *Associated Press,* September 26, 1997.
4. Eric Schoch, "Doctors Offer Tips on Avoiding Infant Deaths," *Indianapolis Star,* June 16, 1995.
5. N.J. Shears, *Infant Suffocation Project—Final Report*, U.S. Consumer Product Safety Commission, January 1995.
6. "Parent's Love Affects Child's Health," *Reuters,* March 10, 1997.
7. David Elkind, *The Hurried Child* (Reading, MA: Addison-Wesley, 1981).
8. Harvard University Preschool Project directed by Dr. Burton White, 1965–1975.

Chapter 24: Parenting Teens

1. Adapted from Erma Bombeck, "Fragile Strings Join Parent, Child," *Arizona Republic,* May 15, 1977.
2. Charles Neider, *The Autobiography of Mark Twain* (New York: Harper Perennial, 1990).
3. Isaiah 53:6.

Chapter 25: Priorities

1. "White House Attorney Found Dead," *Associated Press,* July 20, 1993.
2. "Reflections by Vincent Foster on Law and His Life," *National Law Journal*, August 23, 1993, p. 31.

3. Gary Smith, "Ali and His Entourage," *Sports Illustrated*, April 16, 1988, pp. 48-49.

4. "Courage Performed Outside the Olympics by Its Athletes," *CBS Evening News*, February 8, 1998.

Chapter 26: Self-Esteem and Self-Respect

1. John Bartlett, *Familiar Quotations*, ed. Justin Kaplan, 16th ed. (Boston: Little, Brown and Company, 1992), p. 654.

2. William Manchester, *The Death of a President* (New York: HarperCollins, 1988).

3. Bonnie Miller Rubin, "Taking Showers at School Is Going Down the Drain," *Chicago Tribune*, March 26, 1996.

Chapter 27: Sex, Dating, and Purity

1. Elise F. Jones and Jacqueline Darroch Forest, "Contraceptive Failure in the United States: Revised Estimates from the 1982 National Survey of Family Growth," *Family Planning Perspectives* (21), May/June 1989, p. 103.

2. Ibid., 105.

3. "Factors Associated with Human Papillomavirus Infection in Women Encountered in Community-Based Offices," Barbara Reed, *Archives of Family Medicine*, vol. 2, December 1993, p. 1239.

4. "Genital HPV Infection in Female University Students as Determined by a PCR-Based Method," Heidi M. Bauer, *Journal of the American Medical Association*, vol. 265, no. 472, p. 1991.

5. *Final Report of the Attorney General's Commission on Pornography* (Nashville: Rutledge Hill Press, 1987).

6. Harriet Chiang and Ramon G. McLeod, "Net Porn Law Shot Down," *San Francisco Chronicle*, June 27, 1997.

7. *Fatal Addiction*, Focus on the Family Films, 1989.

8. Desmond Morris, *Intimate Behavior*, rev. ed. (New York: Kodansha America, 1997), pp. 72-103.

Chapter 30: Stress

1. L.M. Boyd, *Boyd's Book of Odd Facts* (New York: Signet, 1980), p. 93.

Chapter 31: Support and Security

1. "The Family at the End of the 20th Century," *Focus on the Family*, June 8-9, 1995.

2. Ronald Kotulak, "Children's Brains May Change in Response to Stress," *Washington Post*, August 31, 1993.

Chapter 32: Trials

1. David Herbert Donald, *Lincoln* (New York: Touchstone Books, 1995).

2. Dennis Overbye, "The Wizard of Space and Time," *Omni*, February 1979, p. 46.

3. Copyright © 1932 by Julia S. Field.

4. *East Gate Newsletter*, April 1997.

5. Max Lucado, *In the Eye of the Storm: A Day in the Life of Jesus* (Dallas: Word, 1991), p. 11.

6. National Park Service, "Battle at Antietam, September 17, 1862," *Civil War Summaries by Campaign*. http://www2.cr.nps.gov/abpp/battles/md003.htm.

Chapter 33: Understanding Your Child

1. Thomas J. Bouchard, et al., "Sources of Human Psychological Differences: The Minnesota Study of Twins Reared Apart," *Science*, October 12, 1990, p. 223.

2. "Twins Separated at Birth: The Story of Jim Lewis and Jim Springer," *Smithsonian* (October 1980).

3. Stella Chess and Alexander Thomas, *Know Your Child: An Authoritative Guide for Today's Parents* (New York: Basic Books, 1987), p. 33.

4. David Swoap, president of Hope Unlimited, telephone conversation with Craig Osten, assistant to author, 1995.

5. Peter Blackburn, "Homeless Children Killed in Brazil," *Reuters*, March 3, 1992.

INDEX